United States
Department of
Agriculture

Forest Service

**Northern
Research Station**

General Technical
Report NRS-18

Measurement Guidelines for the Sequestration of Forest Carbon

Timothy R.H. Pearson
Sandra L. Brown
Richard A. Birdsey

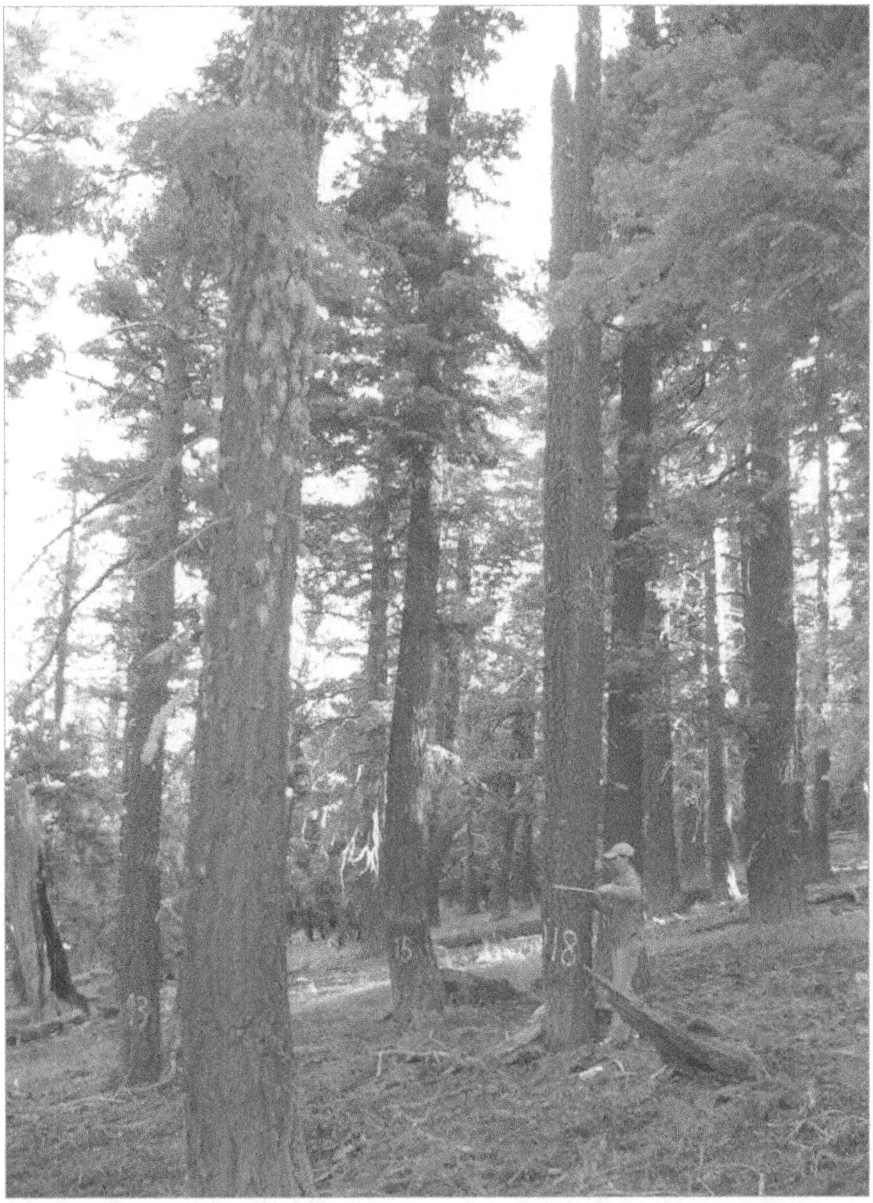

Abstract

Measurement guidelines for forest carbon sequestration were developed to support reporting by public and private entities to greenhouse gas registries. These guidelines are intended to be a reference for designing a forest carbon inventory and monitoring system by professionals with a knowledge of sampling, statistical estimation, and forest measurements. This report provides guidance on defining boundaries; measuring, monitoring, and estimating changes in carbon stocks; implementing plans to measure and monitor carbon; and developing quality assurance and quality control plans to ensure credible and reproducible estimates of the carbon credits. Expected users include entities, e.g., individual landowners, industrial forestry companies and managers of utility company lands, within the United States who are interested in implementing forestry activities and projects designed to generate carbon credits that could be traded as an offset, or for registering carbon dioxide reductions using the U.S. Department of Energy 1605(b) voluntary reporting registry.

The Authors

TIMOTHY R.H. PEARSON and SANDRA L. BROWN are scientists with Winrock International, Washington, D.C.

RICHARD A. BIRDSEY is a program manager with the Northern Research Station at Newtown Square, Pennsylvania.

Cover Photo

Forest measurement in Lake County, Oregon, used with permission from Winrock International.

This publication was sponsored by the USDA Forest Service's Northern Global Change Research Program. We thank David Shoch, Matt Delaney, Mike Amacher, David Chojnacky, Coeli Hoover, and Greg Reams for contributions to an earlier version of this report that is part of the guidelines for the United States Voluntary Reporting of Greenhouse Gases Program. We also thank Jennifer Jenkins, John Stanovick, Jim Cathcart, and Raymond Czaplewski for helpful comments and suggestions. Material presented here does not represent the policy of the sponsoring agency.

CONTENTS

INTRODUCTION AND SCOPE OF GUIDELINES

Measurement guidelines for forest carbon sequestration were developed to support reporting by public and private entities to greenhouse gas registries. Although developed primarily for reporting about forestry "activities"—the categories of actions comprising forestry—rather than "projects", which are specific carbon management undertakings, the guidelines are based on experience with methods for the latter and thus are broadly useful for carbon estimation. The national greenhouse gas registry, known as 1605(b) in reference to the original authorizing language contained in the Energy Policy Act of 1992, accepts reports by entities about their forestry activities as a bundle (Birdsey 2006). Other greenhouse gas registries, such as that maintained by the state of California, accept reports about specific forestry projects.

These guidelines are intended to be a reference for designing a forest carbon inventory and monitoring system, and are based on the authors' experience and the literature. Users should carefully review the material presented here and adapt the recommended procedures to their specific circumstances using local knowledge of forest conditions and practices, and location-specific data where possible. The guidelines are designed for "average" or typical conditions, so your results might not be as precise as described in this report. For example, although our guidelines recommend using generalized biomass equations that represent average national conditions, these equations may not perform well for populations of forest trees that deviate significantly from the average.

These guidelines are designed for use by professionals with a knowledge of sampling, statistical estimation, and forest measurements. Users also should be familiar with specific protocols required by the registry to which the forest-carbon estimates will be reported. We cannot guarantee that a specific application will be accepted by a greenhouse gas registry. Nonetheless, by carefully referencing these guidelines and other sources of information, reporters can meet targeted levels of precision.

Expected users include entities, e.g., individual landowners, industrial forestry companies and managers of utility company lands, within the United States who are interested in implementing forestry activities and projects designed to generate reductions in atmospheric carbon dioxide (CO_2) that could be traded as an offset, or reported to the U.S. Department of Energy 1605(b) voluntary reporting registry. This report provides guidance on defining boundaries; measuring, monitoring, and estimating changes in carbon stocks; implementing plans to measure and monitor carbon; and developing quality assurance and quality control plans to ensure credible and reproducible estimates of the carbon credits.

Forestry activities primarily affect the exchange of CO_2 between the land and atmosphere. Techniques and methods for measuring and monitoring terrestrial carbon pools that are based on commonly accepted principles of forest inventory, soil sampling, and ecological surveys are described in the sections that follow.

Although the primary purpose of forestry activities for greenhouse gas reduction is to increase carbon stocks, these activities also can result in changes in non-CO_2 greenhouse gas emissions and removals.

Examples include burning biomass; applying synthetic and organic fertilizers to soils; cultivating nitrogen-fixing trees; and peat flooding and drainage activities. In addition, land-use activities that disturb soils, e.g., site preparation during afforestation, may affect non-CO_2 emissions and removals from soils. It is likely that these are insignificant in the forest sector, and practical and cost-efficient methods for measuring non-CO_2 greenhouse gases for forestry activities are less well developed. We do not provide guidelines for monitoring, estimating, or reporting significant fluxes of non-CO_2 gases for forestry.

For forestry activities it is not always necessary to measure all carbon pools (Brown et al. 2000). Selective or partial accounting systems may be appropriate so long as all pools for which emissions are likely to increase as a result of the activity (loss in carbon or emission) are included. The selection of which pools to measure and monitor depends on factors such as the expected rate of change, magnitude and direction of the change, availability and accuracy of methods to quantify change, and cost to measure. All pools that are expected to decrease must be measured and monitored. Pools that are expected to increase by a small amount need not be estimated if costs are high relative to the magnitude of the increase. For example, in the case of afforestation, understory herbaceous vegetation rarely is a significant factor in the ecosystem carbon budget.

Our guidelines focus on forest ecosystem carbon only and include only the carbon pools on the land, e.g., live and dead above- and below-ground biomass and soil. The following steps are needed to produce credible and transparent estimates of net changes in carbon stocks:

1. A monitoring plan, including delineation of boundaries, stratification of project area, type and number of sample plots, duration of project, and frequency of monitoring.
2. Sampling procedures for carbon stocks.
3. Methods for estimating carbon stocks and techniques for analyzing the results.
4. Methods for estimating net change in carbon stocks.
5. A quality assurance/quality control plan.

The primary focus is on field measurements designed to produce accurate estimates of net changes in carbon stocks to known levels of precision. A suggested target for the precision for forest-carbon accounting is a sufficient sample of measurements to conclude that with 95-percent confidence, the true population value lies within plus or minus 10 percent of the sample estimate.

Many reporting entities with large tracts of forests have good records on types of management, timber stock, harvest rates, and related information. Such records can be used to develop estimates of net changes in carbon stocks from forestry activities. It is good practice to compare per-acre or per-hectare (ha) estimates with similar estimates from regional databases. For other entities where such data are not available, e.g., for owners of non-industrial forest land, there are numerous national to regional databases that can be downloaded from the internet. Although estimates based on these data likely will be less accurate and less precise than those based on field measurements, such data used in combination with the methods in this report can provide better estimates than those based on default values alone. The following list of web sources are useful for verifying that measurements and calculations are within the ranges reported at national and regional scales.

Internet Sites Available for Carbon Estimation

Internet site:	Organization	Relevant content
http://fia.fs.fed.us/	USDA Forest Service Forest Inventory and Analysis	Forest statistics of the U.S. Forest statistics by state Sample plot and tree data Forest inventory methods and basic definitions
http://www.fhm.fs.fed.us/	USDA Forest Service Forest Health Monitoring	Forest health status Regional data on soils, dead wood stocks Forest health monitoring methods
http://www.usda.gov/oce/global_change/gg_inventory.htm	USDA Greenhouse Gas Inventory	State-by-state forest carbon estimates
http://www.fs.fed.us/ne/durham/4104/index.shtml	USDA Forest Service, U.S. carbon budget project	On-line carbon estimation Forest carbon estimation methods U.S. and regional forest carbon statistics
http://www.fs.fed.us/pnw/sev/rpa/	USDA Forest Service resources planning act	Timber resource statistics and projections
http://unfccc.int/ http://www.ipcc.ch/	United Nations Framework Convention on Climate Change and IPCC	International guidance on carbon accounting and estimation
http://www.wri.org/	World Resources Institute	Greenhouse gas mitigation projects Accounting, measuring, and reporting procedures
http://nature.org/initiatives/climatechange/	The Nature Conservancy	Greenhouse gas mitigation projects Accounting and reporting procedures
http://www.winrock.org/Ecosystems/	Winrock International	Greenhouse gas mitigation projects Developments in baseline and leakage analyses Accounting, measuring, and reporting procedures

MONITORING DESIGN

Boundaries

Forestry activities and the land base for an entity can vary in size (from tens to hundreds of thousands of ha) and can be confined to a single or several geographic areas. The area may be one contiguous block of land with a single owner or many small blocks of land spread over a wide area with numerous small or several large landowners. The spatial boundaries of the land need to be clearly defined to facilitate accurate measuring, monitoring, accounting, and verification. The spatial boundaries can be in the form of permanent boundary markers, e.g., fences; clearly defined topographic descriptions, e.g., rivers/creeks, mountain ridges; spatially explicit boundaries (identified with a Global Positioning System, GPS); and/or other methods. Ground-based surveys that delineate property boundaries are an accurate means of documenting land boundaries. Many methods and tools are available for identifying and delineating land boundaries, including remote sensing, e.g., satellite images from optical or radar sensor systems, aerial photos, GPS, topographic maps, and land records. Larger areas across the landscape can be defined by specific boundary descriptions using GPS-based coordinates on topographic maps or other suitable means.

Boundaries must be documented properly from the start (mapped and described) and preferably not subject to changes for the duration of the estimation period. Boundary changes must be noted and inclusions and/or exclusions of physical land area must be surveyed using the methods described. This would require adjusting the estimated net emissions or removals of greenhouse gases attributable to the activity or entity.

Stratification of Land Area

Stratification Before Activities Begin

Once the land area has been delineated, it is useful to collect basic information such as land-use history as well as maps of soil, vegetation, and topography. The land for the project can be georeferenced and mapped onto a base map. A geographic information system (GIS) is useful for such an activity. Maps can then be used to stratify the area into more or less homogeneous units (relative to carbon stocks and rates of change in carbon) to increase sampling efficiency.

To facilitate field work and increase the accuracy and precision of measuring and monitoring, divide the area (population of interest) into subpopulations or strata that form relatively homogenous units. Useful tools for defining strata include ground-truthed maps from satellite imagery, aerial photos, and maps of vegetation, soils, or topography. Many of these products are available as GIS data layers, e.g., STATSGO soil maps, USGS Digital Elevation Model, 1992 National Land Cover map, that can be overlain in a GIS to identify possible strata. The key to stratification is to ensure that measurements are more alike within each stratum than in the sample frame as a whole. A GIS can automatically determine stratum size and the size of exclusions or buffer zones.

Remote Sensing Data

Data on remote sensing are useful in designing and implementing measuring and monitoring plans for forest-based carbon activities, for example a land-use map for the area, stratification of the area, land-use history, monitoring of overall performance, and verification that the carbon pool exists.

Selected High Resolution Data Sources for Monitoring Carbon Sequestration Projects

Sensor/ satellite	Spatial resolution	Spectral resolution	Revisit time	Owner	Data
Landsat 5 TM	30 m	VNIR/SWIR	16 days	NASA/USGS	http://edc.usgs.gov
Landsat 7 ETM+	30 m	VNIR/SWIR	17 days	NASA/USGS	http://edc.usgs.gov
EO-1 ALI	30 m	VNIR/SWIR	18 days	NASA	http://edc.usgs.gov
EO-1 Hyperion	30 m	VNIR/SWIR	19 days	NASA	http://edc.usgs.gov
IKONOS	1- 4 m	VNIR/SWIR	2 – 5 days	Space Imaging	http://www.spaceimaging.com
Quickbird	0.6 – 3 m	VNIR/SWIR	1 – 4 days	DigitalGlobe	http://www.digitalglobe.com

TM = Thematic Mapper; ETM+ = Enhanced Thematic Mapper Plus; ALI = Advanced Land Imager; VNIR = Visible to Near Infrared; SWIR = Shortwave Infrared

The size and spatial distribution of the land area does not influence site stratification. One large, contiguous block of land or many small parcels can be considered the population of interest and are stratified in the same manner. When an area is not homogeneous, stratification generally reduces monitoring costs, e.g., the amount of sampling required is reduced due to the smaller variation in carbon stocks in each stratum. Stratification should be carried out using criteria that are directly related to the variables to be measured and monitored, for example, the carbon pools in trees for afforestation. For afforestation, the strata can be defined on the basis of variables such as the tree species (if several), age class (as generated by delay in practical planting schedules), initial vegetation (totally cleared versus cleared with patches or scattered trees), and site factors (soil type, elevation, slope, etc.). However, there is a tradeoff between the number of strata and sampling intensity. Strata should be sufficiently large to enable adequate sampling within each stratum but not so large as to incur higher costs.

Site visits to the project area and nearby areas with existing vegetation that will be the target of the activity will aid in stratifying the area. Field assessments and measurements of key variables such as general soil type, topography, and nearby existing vegetation aid in stratification and contribute to cost-effective monitoring.

Post-Stratification

For some areas, it may not be possible to prestratify because the site appears to be homogeneous. However, it is possible that after the first monitoring period, the estimated change in carbon stocks is highly variable within a stratum, and that the original stratum can be subdivided into homogeneous areas (post-stratification).

Type and Number of Sampling Plots

Plot type

For forestry activities, permanent or temporary sampling plots can be used for sampling over time to estimate changes in the relevant carbon pools. Permanent plots are applicable only where both the trees and the plots are permanently marked. For all other pools, temporary plots are used. For trees, both methods have advantages and disadvantages. Permanent sample plots in which trees are tagged generally are regarded as statistically more efficient for estimating changes in forest-carbon stocks than temporary plots because there is high covariance between observations at successive sampling events (Avery and Burkhart 1983). Moreover, the use of permanent plots allows efficient verification at relatively low cost. A verifying organization can find and measure permanent plots at random to verify the design and implementation of the carbon monitoring plan in quantitative terms. Disadvantages of permanent plots are that their location might be known and they might be treated differently, e.g., fertilized or irrigated to enhance the carbon stocks, tags can become dislocated from trees, or they can be destroyed or lost by disturbances over the measurement interval. Advantages of temporary plots are that they can be established more cost-effectively to estimate the carbon stocks of the relevant pools, their location changes at each sampling interval, and they would not be lost to disturbances. The primary disadvantage of temporary plots is related to the precision in estimating the change in forest-carbon stocks. Because individual trees are not tracked (see Clark et al. 2001), the covariance term is nonexistent so it will be more difficult to attain the targeted precision level without measuring more plots. Thus, any time advantage gained by using temporary versus permanent forest plots may be lost by the need to install additional temporary plots to attain the targeted precision.

If permanent sample plots are used it is necessary to mark or map the trees to measure the growth of individuals at each time interval so that growth of survivors, mortality, and ingrowth of new trees can be tracked. Changes in carbon stocks for each tree are then estimated and summed per plot. Statistical analyses are performed on net carbon accumulation per plot, including ingrowth and losses due to mortality. Because permanent plots also track mortality, they can be used to track the major changes in dead wood (both on the ground and standing) after the initial inventory of this component.

Tagging Trees in Permanent Plots

When estimating change in carbon stocks, an important consideration is accounting for ingrowth and mortality. Not understanding where, when, and how to include these components can result in erroneous estimates of changes in the carbon stocks of trees. Here we emphasize why it is important to tag and track individual surviving trees as well as new ingrown trees. For measuring the live-tree pool, there is no requirement to track mortality (measured as part of dead wood pool) but there must be an estimate of trees growing into the plots, i.e., exceeding the minimum measurement size only at time 2.

Figure 1 shows the same trees being measured in a plot that tags and tracks individual trees and in a plot that does not tag or track trees. The change in biomass stock for ingrowth trees is the biomass of the new tree at time 2 minus the minimum biomass required for a tree to be measured (assume four units of biomass in Figure 1).

It is clear that the two methods produce widely different results. Although in this example the untagged plot gives a negative change in stock, it could just as readily give a larger positive change

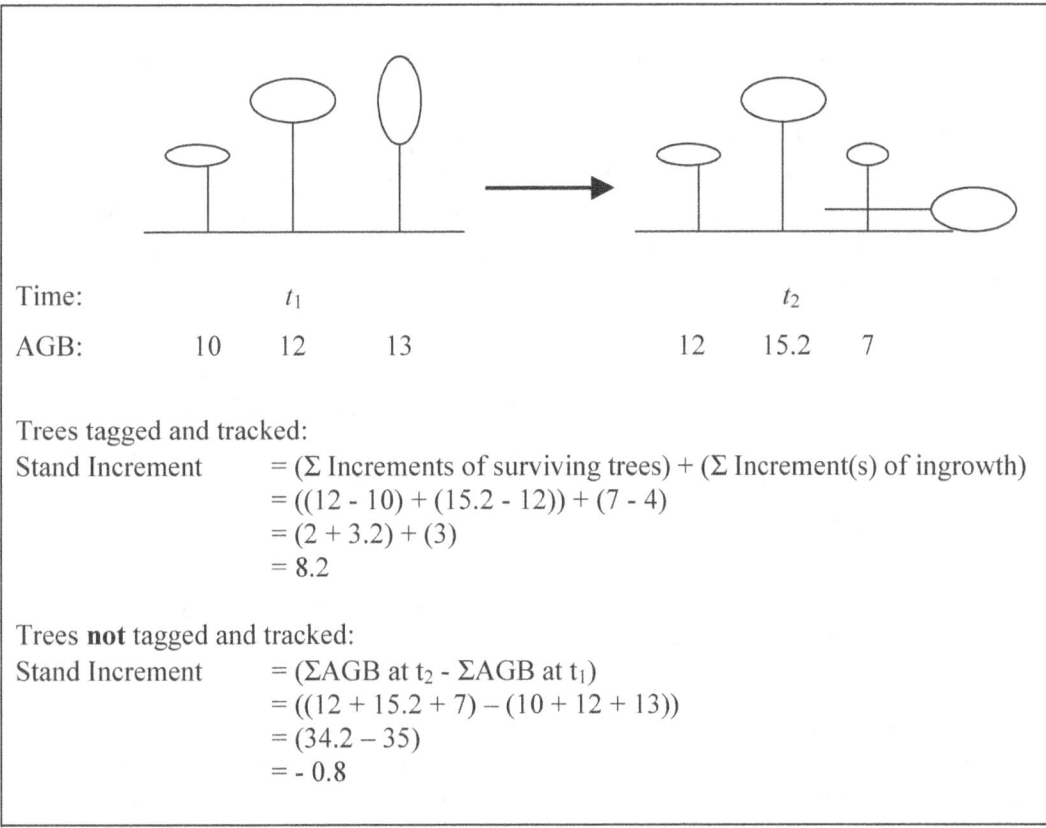

Time: t_1 t_2

AGB: 10 12 13 12 15.2 7

Trees tagged and tracked:

Stand Increment
$$= (\Sigma \text{ Increments of surviving trees}) + (\Sigma \text{ Increment(s) of ingrowth})$$
$$= ((12 - 10) + (15.2 - 12)) + (7 - 4)$$
$$= (2 + 3.2) + (3)$$
$$= 8.2$$

Trees **not** tagged and tracked:

Stand Increment
$$= (\Sigma AGB \text{ at } t_2 - \Sigma AGB \text{ at } t_1)$$
$$= ((12 + 15.2 + 7) - (10 + 12 + 13))$$
$$= (34.2 - 35)$$
$$= -0.8$$

Figure 1.—Illustration of the methods for calculating change in above-ground biomass stocks for trees that are or are not tagged and tracked in permanent plots. AGB = above-ground biomass of live trees; AGB of a minimum-size tree is set arbitrarily to 4 units (based on Clark et al. 2001).

than the tagged plots. Because individual trees are not tracked in the untagged plots, there is no way of knowing that the 7-unit tree at t_2 was ingrowth or that the 13-unit tree at t_1 died during the interval.

Prism Plots

The alternative to fixed-area plots is point sampling using basal area prisms (point sampling). When a prism from a fixed point is used, trees are tallied according to size. Tree stems at diameter at breast height (d.b.h.) that are close enough to completely fill the sighting angle are tallied. Stems that are too small or too distant are ignored.

The primary advantage of point sampling is the speed with which data are collected, i.e., no fixed-plot boundary is involved. However, errors in the tallies arising from point sampling are more serious than those arising from fixed-area plots. Because point sampling preferentially samples large trees, it is well suited to commercial forestry and to rapid reconnaissance sampling, though sampling with fixed-area plots generally is more precise (Avery and Burkhart 1994) and representative of the full range of trees that contribute to carbon estimation.

Number of Plots, Precision, and Sample Size

Because the level of precision required for a carbon inventory has a direct effect on inventory costs, it must be carefully chosen by users of inventory results. A reasonable estimate of the net change in carbon stocks that can be achieved at a reasonable cost is to target within 10 percent of the true value of the mean at the 95-percent confidence level (see Brown 2002).

When the level of precision has been chosen, sample sizes must be determined for each stratum in the project area. Each carbon pool will have a different variance (amount of variation around the mean). However, focusing on the variance of the tree component for forestry activities captures most of the total variance. Although the variance in other pools may be high, it often contributes little to the net change in carbon stocks or it can reduce the total variance when the net change in all pools is estimated. For example, the understory in forests can be highly variable but it usually is a negligible component of the net change. By contrast, dead wood, though highly variable, often reduces the overall variability of the net change in carbon. Soils often are the exception. Soil-carbon stocks are highly variable and are less closely associated with tree carbon stocks than the other measurement pools. It is advisable to have a sampling scheme specifically for soils if they are an important component of the anticipated carbon benefits.

The sample size for monitoring in each stratum must be calculated on the basis of the estimated variance of the carbon stock (between separate measurement plots) in each stratum, and the proportional area of the stratum. Typically, to estimate the number of plots needed for monitoring at a given confidence level, one must first obtain an estimate of the expected variance of the carbon stock in each stratum. This can be accomplished from existing data of the type of activity to be implemented, e.g., a forest inventory in an area representative of the proposed activity, or by taking measurements on an existing area that represents the proposed activity. For example, if the activity is to afforest agricultural lands and it will last for 20 years, a measure of the carbon stocks of approximately 15 plots of an existing 20-year forest would suffice. If the project area comprises more than one stratum, repeat this procedure for each one. Such measurements will provide estimates of the variance in each stratum and, along with the area of the stratum, the total number of plots per stratum can be estimated by standard statistical methods.

As sampling plots cannot always be relocated or reoccupied for a variety of reasons, for example, if plot markers are overgrown or removed by people, plots are burned, or records are lost, it is prudent to increase the number of plots beyond the minimum in the initial sampling design. Increasing the number of plots to some percentage over the calculated minimum number of samples provides a cushion that helps meet minimum precision requirements despite missing plots in subsequent inventories. The minimum sample size should be increased by at least 10 percent to allow for plots that cannot be relocated or are lost due to unforeseen circumstances.

Managers who contemplate progressive plantings over time must develop an open-ended monitoring framework that can accommodate the progressive addition of plantings to the area over time. This can be done by predicting the eventual size of the area at year X and progressively assigning distinct stand-age cohorts to separate strata within the overall population, anticipating that a full contingent of permanent sample plots would be installed by year X. No more than two or three age classes should be combined into one cohort class.

Using Forest Inventory and Analysis Data to Estimate Coefficient of Variation and Number of Sampling Plots

- Download data (http://ncrs2.fs.fed.us/4801/fiadb/) and apply biomass equations and expansion factors (see section 4.1) for the specific area and forest type of interest. Sum to obtain plot level results.
- Calculate mean carbon stocks across the dataset or optionally across strata of interest, then calculate standard deviation and the coefficient of variation.
- The minimum number of plots required for monitoring is calculated by solving for n in the formula for the confidence interval (CI). Target ± 7 to 8 percent of the mean as a reasonable level of precision (this accounts for the sampling error only; sources of error such as measurement error and model error likely will account for 10 to 20 percent of total error thus, a target of ± 7 to 8 percent CI of the mean for sampling will result in a total error for the confidence interval of about 10 percent of the mean).

$$n = (s \times 2.1)/(\text{mean} \times 0.08)^2 \qquad (\text{where } s = \text{standard deviation})$$

The 95 percent CI becomes the ±8 percent precision chosen—i.e. we can be 95 percent confident that the true mean is covered by the determined sampling precision.

- If the activity is planned to run for 50 to 70 years, use the large FIA size class (one method of sorting FIA data) where variation and consequently minimum number of plots is low. Variation is highest in young or small size-class plots regardless of whether regeneration was natural or artificial.
- The minimum number of plots can be decreased by stratification of study area, for example, by slope, soil type, or site index.

Coefficients of variation ([standard deviation * 100] / mean) and minimum number of sampling plots at 95 percent confidence level calculated for specific forest types in three regions using FIA data.

Region	Forest type	FIA size class	Percent C.V.	Number of plots (95 percent)
Ohio	Oak-hickory	Large	27	45
		Medium	33	65
		Small	63	237
Illinois	Oak-hickory	Large	41	99
		Medium	35	74
		Small	74	325
Lower Mississippi Valley	Bottomlands	Large	29	50
		Medium	33	66
		Small	80	384

At the simplest level, the number of plots required should be calculated using the following equation:

$$n = \left(\frac{ts}{E}\right)^2$$

Where

E = allowable error or the desired half width of the confidence interval. Calculated by multiplying the mean carbon stock by the desired precision, i.e., mean carbon stock * 0.1 (for 10-percent precision) or 0.2 (for 20-percent precision),

t = the sample statistic from the t-distribution for the 95-percent confidence level; t usually is set at 2 as sample size is unknown at this stage,

s = standard deviation of stratum

Where the project is composed of strata, a more complex equation should be used:

For L strata, the number of plots needed (n) =

$$n = \frac{\left(\sum_{h=1}^{L} N_h * s_h\right)^2}{\dfrac{N^2 * E^2}{t^2} + \left(\sum_{h=1}^{L} N_h * s_h^2\right)}$$

This equation can be simplified as:

For a single stratum:

$$n = \frac{(N * s)^2}{\dfrac{N^2 * E^2}{t^2} + N * s^2}$$

For two strata:

$$n = \frac{\left\langle (N_1 * s_1) + (N_2 * s_2) \right\rangle^2}{\dfrac{N^2 * E^2}{t^2} + N_1 * s_1^2 + N_2 * s_2^2}$$

Where

E = allowable error or the desired half width of the confidence interval. Calculated by multiplying the mean carbon stock by the desired precision, i.e., mean carbon stock * 0.1 (for 10-percent precision) or 0.2 (for 20-percent precision),

t = the sample statistic from the t-distribution for the 95-percent confidence level; t usually is set at 2 as sample size is unknown at this stage,

N_h = number of sampling units for stratum h (= area of the stratum, in ha/area of the plot, in ha),

N = number of sampling units in the population ($N = \sum N_h$),

s_h = standard deviation of stratum h

Frequency of monitoring

The frequency of monitoring is related to the rate and magnitude of change. The smaller the expected change, the greater the potential that frequent monitoring will not detect a significant change. This becomes a cost-benefit analysis so that the frequency of monitoring should be determined by the magnitude of expected change. Less frequent monitoring is applicable only if small changes are expected.

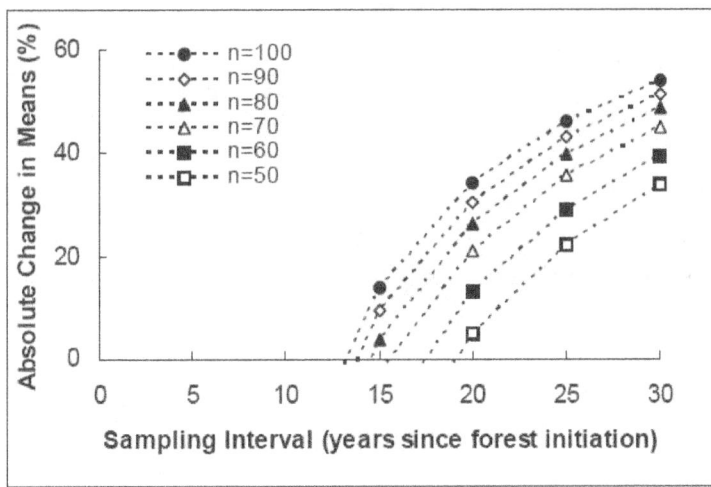

Figure 2.—Example of how percent absolute change in the mean (with 95 percent confidence) soil carbon for afforestation activities varies in relation to the sampling interval and sample size (n), assuming constant coefficient of variation (30 percent), constant rate of soil carbon accumulation of 0.5 t C/ha/yr, and initial soil carbon 50 t/ha.

Increasing the interval between sampling events should increase the magnitude of the change that takes place which, where variance around the means is constant, increases the percentage and magnitude of the change resolved (Fig. 2). This is an important consideration because small changes expected with short sampling intervals may be undetectable, even with high sampling intensity.

Frequency of monitoring should consider the carbon dynamics of the activity and costs involved. Given the dynamics of forest processes, they generally are measured at intervals of 5 years. For carbon pools that respond more slowly, e.g., soil, even longer periods can be used -- perhaps even 20 years between sampling events. Thus for carbon accumulating in the trees, the frequency of measuring and monitoring should be defined in accordance with the rate of change of the carbon stock, or in accordance with the rotation length in the case of plantations.

A disadvantage of long periods between sample events is the risk of natural or anthropogenic disturbance, the effects of which will not be captured with widely spaced monitoring intervals. This needs to be taken into account when deciding on the frequency of monitoring.

Independent checks of the monitoring system are recommended to ensure data quality. Monitoring changes in carbon stocks in the permanent sampling plots does not always provide information that the changes in carbon stocks are the same across the entire area and/or that the purpose of the activity is accomplished, e.g., to establish several thousand hectares of trees. Repeated visits to the carbon-monitoring plots reveal that the carbon in those plots, which were located randomly and purportedly represent the population, is accumulating with known accuracy and precision. To determine that the plots are representative of the entire project area, periodic checks should be made to ensure that the overall activity is performing in the same way as the plots. This is done by field checking indicators of carbon stock changes, e.g., tree height for afforestation activities. Thus, indicators can be produced that can readily be field-checked across the area. High-resolution satellite imagery also can be used to accomplish this task, at least with respect to the area treated. Periodic acquisition of such imagery or even aerial imagery might be a relatively inexpensive way to monitor overall performance.

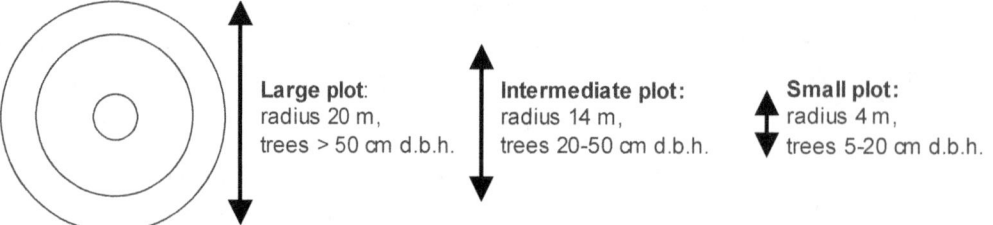

Figure 3.—Schematic of nested, fixed area circular sample plots. The radius and diameter limits for each circular plot would be a function of local conditions and expected size of the trees through time.

SAMPLING DESIGN

Plot Layout

Permanent plot locations can be selected randomly or systematically (plot grid). If plot values are distributed irregularly in a random pattern, both approaches are about equally precise. If some parts of the strata have a higher carbon content than others, systematic selection usually results in greater precision than random selection. Systematic sampling also may appear more credible. The risk is that a map of random sample locations might seem like the plots were selected to monitor only high-carbon areas. Systematic samples are incontrovertible. Sample locations can be readily defined by GIS for either approach.

Size and Shape of Sample Plots

The size and shape of the sample plots is a tradeoff among accuracy, precision, and time (cost) of measurement. Sample plots containing smaller subunits of various shapes and sizes are cost effective depending on the variables to be measured. For example, for afforestation, all trees are measured in the entire sample plot, whereas data on nontree vegetation, litter, and soil are collected in a smaller sub-plot. The FIA standard plot consists of a cluster of four subplots, each containing smaller nested plots for sampling understory vegetation and soils, of relatively small radius.

Unlike fixed-area plots (Fig. 3), nested plots are better suited to stands with a wide range of tree diameters or to stands with changing diameters and stem densities. The optimum area for nested plots can be anticipated by predicting changes in stem density and mean stem diameter over time, or by direct measurements of proxy stands of known age. A nested plot design is efficient when it it likely that individual trees will grow at different rates resulting in *uneven size* distribution. However, if the forest is likely to remain *even-sized,* a single-size plot would suffice. For example, limited-duration afforestation or highly managed short rotation plantations require only a single-size plot.

Nested plots are composed of several full circular or rectangular plots; each nested plot should be viewed separately. The number of nested circles or rectangles depends on forest structure and the length of the activity. Where the activity is to plant trees but to track only for 20 years, a single-size plot likely would suffice. However, additional nested circles or rectangles should be added beyond this duration; a diverse mature forest might require four plot sizes. When trees attain the minimum size for one of the nested circles, they are measured and included. When they exceed the maximum size, measurement of the tree in that nest stops and begins in the next larger nest. If ingrowth into a new nest occurs between censuses, the growth up to the maximum size is included with the smaller nest. Growth in excess of this size is accounted for in the larger nest.

Plot Size

Time and effort spent on field measurements depends on sample size (number of plots) and plot area. Although increasing sample size increases precision, increasing plot area reduces variability between plots roughly following the relationship derived and discussed by Freese (1962). By increasing plot area, variation between plots is reduced, allowing for a smaller sample size while achieving the same precision level. For example, pilot studies can provide an estimate of the CV and plot area (e.g., from FIA plots). Then a plot size can be selected to achieve the desired precision and cost considerations. However, calculating a new plot size for each strata is an added cost and introduces a complexity that can result in additional measurement errors. It is common to select a standard constant plot size (see Figure 3), which balances measurement effort and variability of plot-level results.

Plots are extrapolated to the full-hectare area to produce carbon-stock estimates. Extrapolation by use of expansion factors occurs by calculating the proportion of a hectare that is occupied by a given plot. For example, if a series of nested circles measuring 4, 14, and 20 m in radius were used, their areas equal 50, 616 and 1,257 m^2 respectively. The expansion factors for converting the plot data to a hectare basis are 198.9 for the smallest, 16.2 for the intermediate, and 8.0 for the largest nested circular plot (1 ha = 10,000 m^2).

Selecting Carbon Pools to Measure and Monitor

The key pools included in forestry activities are defined in Table 1. Selecting which pool to measure and monitor depends on several factors, including expected rate of change, magnitude and direction of the change, availability and accuracy of methods to quantify change, and cost to measure. All pools that are expected to decrease significantly due to activities must be measured and monitored. The 1605(b) process includes a *de minimis* criterion whereby any emission that is equal to or less than 3 percent of the total need not be monitored. Moreover, it generally is not cost effective to monitor pools that are expected to change by a small amount relative to the overall rate of change, e.g., understory herbaceous vegetation in the case of an afforestation project. The decision matrix in

Table 1.—Key carbon pools for forests and their definition

Carbon Pool	Definition
Live trees	Live trees: above ground Live trees: below ground
Understory vegetation	Tree seedlings Shrubs, herbs, forbs, grasses
Standing dead trees	Standing dead trees: above ground Standing dead trees: below ground
Down dead wood	Down dead wood Stumps and dead roots
Forest floor	Fine woody debris Litter Humus
Soil carbon	Soil carbon
Wood products	Harvested wood mass

Table 2.—Decision matrix illustrates selection of pools to measure and monitor in forestry projects that can be implemented in the United States (modified from Brown et al. 2000)

| Activity | Living biomass | | | Dead organic matter | | Soil | Wood products[a] |
	Above-ground tree	Above-ground nontree	Below-ground	Forest floor	Dead wood		
Afforestation	Y1	M2	Y3	M4	M5	Y6	M
Forest restoration	Y1	M2	Y3	M4	M5	Y6	N
Forest management	Y1	N	Y3	M4	Y5	N	Y
Agroforestry	Y1	M2	Y3	M4	N	Y6	M
Short-rotation biomass energy plantations	Y1	N	Y3	M4	N	Y6	Y
Mine-land reclamation	Y1	M2	Y3	M4	M5	Y6	M
Forest preservation	Y1	M2	Y3	M4	M5	M6	Y

[a] No methods are provided for measuring this pool as the focus of this report is on ecosystem carbon; see http://treesearch.fs.fed.us/pubs/22954 for methods for estimating change in stocks of wood products.

Letters in table refer to the need for measuring and monitoring carbon pools

Y =   Yes: the change in this pool likely will be large and should be measured.
N =   No: the change likely will be small to none so it is not necessary to measure this pool.
M =   Maybe: the change in this pool might require measuring depending on the forest type and/or management intensity of the project.

Numbers in table refer to different methods for measuring and monitoring carbon pools:

1 =   See methods of carbon-stock measurement for above-ground biomass of trees.
2 =   See methods described for above-ground biomass of nontree vegetation.
3 =   See methods for measuring/estimating the carbon stock in below-ground biomass.
4 =   See methods for measuring carbon stock in forest floor.
5 =   See methods for measuring dead wood.
6 =   See methods for measuring carbon pool in soils.

Table 2 shows the primary carbon pools for forests and which ones should be (Y), might be (M), or should not be (N) measured for each type of forestry activity.

Clearly, it makes sense to measure and monitor the carbon pool in live trees and their roots for all activity types. Above-ground nontree biomass or understory vegetation might require measuring if this is a significant component, e.g., where shrubs are dominant or codominant with other forms of vegetation. Measuring might not be required if the understory is dominated by herbaceous material as this likely would account for negligible changes over the duration of the activity (less than 3 percent). The forest floor should be measured for most activity types, particularly where the forest likely will be dominated by conifers, as this can be a significant component of the total carbon pool.

Dead wood consists of standing dead trees and downed dead wood. For changes in management for timber, this must be measured as this pool often decreases as a result of a project. For example, the change from more intensive to less intensive harvesting causes the dead-wood pool to decrease (less timber is removed and less slash is left behind).

For the preservation of mature forests, it can be expected that substantial emissions will result in the baseline. Soil organic carbon likely will change significantly for afforestation, forest restoration, and mine-land reclamation as the initial amount of soil carbon likely will be low. However, changes in forest management or even forest preservation (from harvesting to preservation) likely will produce very small or undetectable changes in soil carbon, and the cost to measure this pool might exceed the value of the carbon.

The decision to monitor wood products depends on whether the project will be harvested. For short-rotation biomass energy plantations, monitoring would be required as the product is the primary purpose of the activity. Activities related to changes in forest management also require monitoring of wood products as harvesting often changes the live carbon pool. The same is true for forest preservation if the original activity was timber production. In other words, all of the live biomass that is "protected" by the activity (as preservation or reduced logging intensity) cannot be claimed as a savings for the atmosphere because some biomass went into long-term wood products.

MEASUREMENT AND DATA ANALYSIS TECHNIQUES

Measurements of net carbon flows for forests generally lend themselves to the stock-change method, that is, the amount of carbon sequestered is estimated as the net change in carbon stocks over time. Much of the previous discussion focused on the design required to estimate changes in carbon stocks precisely. Although the stock change method is applicable for most components, the flow method may be appropriate for some components. For example, changes in the dead wood pool often are estimated from the difference between inputs from slash (estimated from the difference between total tree biomass and mass of timber removed) and outputs from decomposition of the dead wood. In the sections that follow, both the stock and flow approaches are described where applicable.

These methods are based on measurements and models resulting in estimates of biomass except for soil, which can be measured directly in units of carbon. Biomass always is oven dried and generally is converted to units of carbon by multiplying biomass by 0.5 (the 1605b and Intergovernmental Panel on Climate Change default), unless more specific data are available.

Living Above-ground Biomass

Trees

The carbon stocks of trees are estimated most accurately and precisely by direct methods, e.g., through a field inventory, where all the trees in the sample plots above a minimum diameter are measured. The minimum diameter often is 5 cm in d.b.h., but it can vary depending on the expected size of trees. For arid environments in which trees grow slowly, the minimum d.b.h. may be as small as 2.5 cm; for humid environments in which trees grow rapidly, the minimum d.b.h. may be up to 10 cm. Biomass and carbon stock are estimated using appropriate allometric equations applied to the tree measurements. Tree biomass often is estimated from equations that relate biomass to d.b.h. only. Although the combination of d.b.h. and height as the independent variables is often superior to d.b.h. alone, measuring tree height can be time consuming and will increase the cost of a monitoring program. Further, the empirical database of trees in the United States shows that highly significant biomass regression equations can be developed using d.b.h. only (Tables 3 - 4).

Biomass equations often are reported for individual species or groups of species, but the literature is inconsistent and/or incomplete for all U.S. tree species. However, recent analyses have shown that

Table 3.—Parameters and equations[a] for estimating total above-ground biomass for hardwood and softwood species grouped in 10 classes in the United States. (Jenkins et al. 2004.)

Species group	Parameter β_0	Parameter β_1	Data points[b]	Max[c] d.b.h.	RMSE[d]	R^2
				cm	*log units*	
Hardwood						
Aspen/alder/ Cottonwood/ willow	-2.2094	2.3867	230	70	0.507441	0.953
Soft maple/birch	-1.9123	2.3651	316	66	0.491685	0.958
Mixed hardwood	-2.4800	2.4835	289	56	0.360458	0.980
Hard maple/oak/ Hickory/ beech	-2.0127	2.4342	485	73	0.236483	0.988
Softwood						
Cedar/larch	-2.0336	2.2592	196	250	0.294574	0.981
Douglas-fir	-2.2304	2.4435	165	210	0.218712	0.992
True fir/hemlock	-2.5384	2.4814	395	230	0.182329	0.992
Pine	-2.5356	2.4349	331	180	0.253781	0.987
Spruce	-2.0773	2.3323	212	250	0.250424	0.988
Woodland[e]						
Juniper/oak/mesquite	-0.7152	1.7029	61	78	0.384331	0.938

[a]Biomass equation:

$$y = Exp(\beta_0 + \beta_1 Ln\ x)$$

Where

y　= total aboveground biomass (kg) for trees 2.5 cm and larger in d.b.h.,

x　= d.b.h. (cm),

Exp = "e" to the power of,

Ln = *natural log base "e"* (2.718282).

[b]Number of data points generated from published equations (generally at intervals of 5-cm d.b.h.) for parameter estimation.

[c]Maximum d.b.h. of trees measured in published equations; beyond this maximum diameter equations should only be used with caution.

[d]Root mean squared error or estimate of the standard deviation of the regression error term in natural log units.

[e]Woodland group includes both hardwood and softwood species from dry-land forests.

Table 4.—Parameters and equations[a] for estimating above-ground biomass for southern and eastern hardwood and softwood species in the United States (from Brown and Schroeder 1999)

Species class	Parameter β_0	Parameter β_1	Parameter β_2	Parameter β_3	Number of data points	Max d.b.h.	R^2
						cm	
Hardwood	0.5	25000	2.5	246872	454	85.1	0.990
Pine	0.887	10486	2.84	376907	137	56.1	0.980
Fir-spruce	0.357	34185	2.47	425676	83	71.6	0.980

[a]Biomass equation:

$$y = \beta_0 + \frac{\beta_1 x^{\beta_2}}{x^{\beta_2} + \beta_3}$$

Where

　y = above-ground biomass (kg),

　x = d.b.h. (cm).

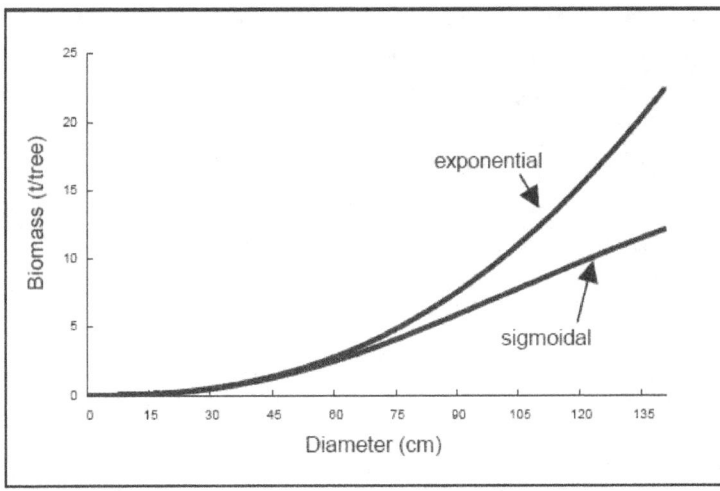

Figure 4.—Comparison of the relative treatment of large trees by equations with an exponential form, e.g., the hard maple/oak/hickory/beech equation; Table 3, and those with a limiting function, e.g., the eastern hardwoods equation; Table 4.

equations based on multi-species groupings can work well for U.S. forests (Schroeder et al. 1997; Jenkins et al. 2004).

Jenkins et al. (2004) compiled all available diameter-based allometric regression equations for estimating total above-ground and component biomass, defined in terms of dry mass, for U.S. trees. More than 1,700 biomass equations were assembled for more than 100 species from 177 sources. Using a subset of 318 equations from 104 sources, Jenkins et al. (2003) developed generalized equations appropriate for estimating tree biomass from d.b.h. at large scales. This approach for generalized equations included a method for generating "pseudodata" (Pastor et al. 1984) by calculating biomass values for a range of diameters within bounds of raw data for each equation. These pseudodata were used to refit new equations for 10 broad species groups (Table 3). See Jenkins et al. (2003) for details on species in each group.

When using allometric equations, note carefully the given maximum diameter used in the regression. The equations for trees that exceed the maximum diameters should be used only after considering the functional form of the equation. In particular, caution should be used for equations based on an exponential function beyond the range of diameters used to develop the equation, e.g., the equations in Table 3. Equations with more sigmoidal form, where biomass is constrained at large diameters, can be used with confidence, even beyond the given maximum bounds (Brown et al. 1989). The general equations of Schroeder et al. (1997) and Brown and Schroeder (1999) with this sigmoidal/constrained form are shown in Table 3. The estimated biomass per tree for a given diameter based on the exponential and sigmoidal models is compared in Figure 4. Up to about 75 cm in diameter, the models give the same estimated biomass per tree. Beyond this size, the exponential models show an increasingly larger estimated biomass while the sigmoidal model is more conservative. The maximum diameter used by the authors to create the exponential curve is 73 cm; this is approximately where the two curves diverge significantly.

The equations of Jenkins et al. (2003) exhaustively cover U.S. tree flora, but they are dominated by western species in the softwood category. Western softwoods are unique in stature and thus do not adequately represent southern pines or eastern fir-spruce species. By contrast, the equations of Brown and Schroeder (1999) for pines and fir-spruce (Table 4) are calculated specifically for these species groups. In the following example, above-ground tree biomass is calculated for a plot using allometric regression equations.

Calculating Carbon Stock and its Change in Above-ground Trees from Allometric Regression Equations

In this example, a single plot from an oak-hickory forest is examined. The plot consists of three nested subplots:

- **5-m radius for trees 2.5 to < 10 cm d.b.h.**   *expansion factor: 198.9*
- **14-m radius for trees ≥ 10 to < 50 cm d.b.h.**   *expansion factor: 16.2*
- **20-m radius for trees ≥ 50 cm d.b.h.**   *expansion factor: 8.0*

The allometric regression equation of Jenkins et al. (2003) is used for hard maple/oak/hickory/beech to convert from d.b.h. to biomass.

The following shows measurements over two periods using permanent plots in which all trees are tagged. At time 2, note the ingrowth of trees too small to be measured at time 1 (trees 101 and 102 in the small nest and 103 in the intermediate nest) and the outgrowth from one plot size and ingrowth into the next size when the max/min thresholds are passed (trees 004, 005 small to intermediate, tree 009 intermediate to large). That is, a tree's growth during a given period can be split as follows: outgrowth is accounted for in the plot in which it is growing to the point where its diameter moves it to the larger nested plot, —i.e. where the tree's remaining growth is accounted for as ingrowth for the large plot into which it moved.

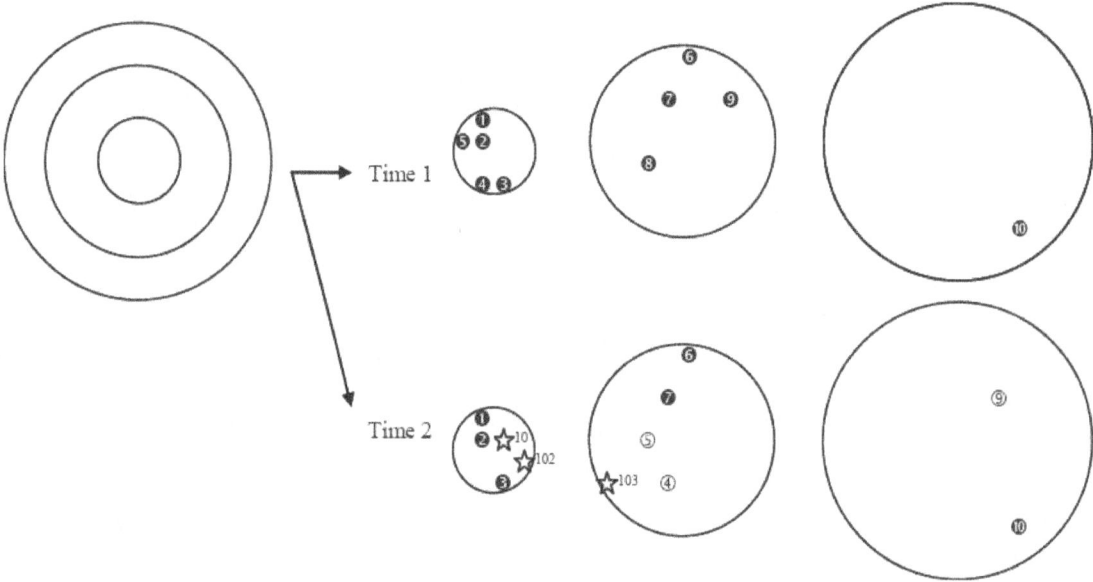

In the figure above the three nested plots are shown at time 1 and time 2. The numbers/stars indicate the position of trees. At time 2, numbers in dark circles indicate trees that remained in the same size class as at time 1. Numbers in other circles indicate trees that have grown into the next class. Stars are trees that have exceeded the measurement minimum for that plot for the first time. The number indicates the tag number in the following table.

Time 1				Time 2			
tag	Nest	D.b.h.	Biomass	tag	Nest	D.b.h.	Biomass
		cm	kg			cm	kg
001	Small	2.6	1.37	001	Small	3.1	2.10
002	Small	5.3	7.74	002	Small	5.8	9.64
003	Small	6.1	10.90	003	Small	6.8	14.20
004	Small	6.2	11.34	004	Intermediate	10	36.32
005	Small	8.1	21.74	005	Intermediate	12.1	57.76
006	Intermediate	10.2	38.11	006	Intermediate	10.9	44.79
007	Intermediate	12.3	60.11	007	Intermediate	13.3	72.71
008	Intermediate	38.6	972.67	008	DEAD	DEAD	972.67
009	Intermediate	48.2	1670.20	009	Large	51	1916.30
010	Large	57.0	2512.15	010	Large	58	2620.79
				101	Small	2.5	1.24
				102	Small	2.8	1.64
				103	Intermediate	10.3	39.03

Change in biomass stocks in each subplot = (Σ biom. increments of trees remaining in subplot size class) + (Σ biom. increments for outgrowth trees [= Σ max biomass for size class – biomass at time 1]) + (Σ biom. increments for ingrowth trees [= Σ biomass at time 2 – min biomass for size class]).

(The numbers in dark circles and squares indicate the tree tag numbers for each increment)

Small subplot = [❶ (2.1-1.37) + ❷ (9.64-7.74) + (❸14.20-10.9)] +
[❹ (36.32-11.34) + ❺ (36.32-21.74)] + [**101** (1.24-1.24) + **102** (1.64-1.24)]

= (0.73 + 1.90 + 3.30) + (24.98 + 14.58) + (0 + 0.49) = 45.89 kg

Intermediate subplot = [❻ (44.79-38.11) + ❼ (72.71-60.11)] + [❾ (1826.12-1670.20)]
+ [❹ (36.32-36.32) + ❺ (57.76-36.32) + **103** (39.03-36.32)]

= (6.68 + 12.60) + (155.92) + (0 + 21.44 + 2.71) = 199.35 kg

Large subplot = (❿ (2620.79-2512.15)) + ((0)) + (❾ (1916.30-1826.12))

= (108.64) + (0) + (90.18) = 198.82 kg

Change in biomass = Σ Δbiomass in each subplot x expansion factor for that subplot

Small = 45.89 x 127.32 = 5,842.71 kg/ha
Int. = 199.35 x 16.24 = 3,237.44 kg/ha
Large = 198.82 x 7.96 = 1,582.13 kg/ha

Sum = 10,662.28 kg/ha = 10.7 t/ha or 5.35 t C/ha (biomass * 0.5) for the time interval

All allometric equations are estimating biomass and as such will have an uncertainty associated with them. The broader the equation in geographic scope and species included, the greater the uncertainty. The uncertainty is indicated by the r^2 value and can be included in the total uncertainty using the root mean square error.

To ensure that there is no systematic bias from the use of regional equations at a local scale, it is good practice to roughly estimate the volume of approximately 10 trees and apply a wood density to obtain biomass, which in turn, should be compared with biomass calculated using an allometric equation. Volume can be estimated by calculating the volume of the trunk of the tree (volume = $1/3\pi$ x h x $[r_1^2 + r_2^2 + r_1 \times r_2]$ where h is the height of the tree, r_1 is the radius at the base of the tree, and r_2 is the estimated radius at the top of the tree), and multiplying this by 1.2 to approximately account for branches and leaves. Biomass is determined by multiplying volume by density.

An alternative approach for estimating the biomass of forests is using the volume of the commercial component of the tree. This volume is estimated with standard forestry techniques. This method is commonly used with temporary plots. The estimated volume must be converted to total above-ground biomass, which includes the other tree components, e.g., branches, twigs, and leaves. The volume method is based on factors developed at the stand level for closed canopy forests. It <u>cannot</u> be used for estimating biomass of individual trees.

There are two potential methods. The first calculates biomass directly from stand volume for different vegetation types in different regions. The second includes the additional step of calculating a biomass expansion factor (BEF). Neither method has a statistical advantage with respect to end results. In both methods, growing-stock volume (GSV) is defined as the net outside bark volume of growing-stock trees at least 12.5 cm in d.b.h. to a minimum of 10 cm in diameter at treetop or the point at which the central stem breaks into limbs (definition used by FIA). Other definitions of volume could be used but the BEFs reported here *could not* be applied—new ones would have to be developed for local conditions.

Direct Method

Smith et al. (2003) used FIA data on growing-stock volume and the biomass equations of Jenkins et al. (2003) to develop regression equations of the form:

Above-ground biomass (t/ha) = F x (G + (1-exp(-GSV (m^3/ha) /H)))

Where

GSV = growing-stock volume,
F, G, H = regression coefficients

Fifty-seven variants of this equation were developed for a variety of forest types across 10 regions in the continental United States. See Smith et al. (2003) for details on the coefficients for each of the variants of the equation (http://www.fs.fed.us/ne/newtown_square/publications/technical_reports/ index.shtml). Schroeder et al. (1997) also used this approach for eastern U.S. hardwood and softwood forests, but developed equations of a different form based on a smaller subset of the FIA database.

20

Biomass Expansion Factor Method

This method is expressed as (Brown and Schroeder 1999):

Above-ground biomass (t/ha) = GSV (m^3/ha) x BEF (t/m^3)

Where

GSV = growing-stock volume,
BEF = [total above-ground biomass of all living trees above a minimum d.b.h. of 2.5 cm]/[growing-stock volume]

The BEF is significantly related to the GSV for most forest types, generally starting high at low volumes and then declining at an exponential rate to a constant low value at high volumes. Thus, using one value for the BEF for all values of GSV is incorrect. This general relationship applies to many of the world's forests, including tropical forests (Brown 1997) and forests in China (Fang et al. 1998).

Schroeder et al. (1997) and Brown and Schroeder (1999) provided methods for calculating the BEF (t/m^3) for all hardwood and softwood forest types and regions across the Eastern United States.

Hardwoods: BEF = exp(1.912 – (0.344 x ln GSV))
              If GSV > 200 m^3/ha use a constant BEF of 1.0

Spruce-Fir: BEF = exp(1.771 - (0.339 x ln GSV))
              If GSV > 160 m^3/ha use a constant BEF of 1.0.

Pines: GSV < 10 m^3/ha   BEF = 1.68 t/m^3
              GSV 10 – 100 m^3/ha   BEF = 0.95 t/m^3
              GSV > 100 m^3/ha   BEF = 0.81 t/m^3

where GSV = growing stock volume in m^3/ha

In the following example, both the direct and the BEF methods are used to calculate biomass for two forest types. The two methods differ by less than 5 percent for both forest types and thus can be considered as giving equivalent results.

Calculating Biomass from Stand Volume Data

Example 1: An oak-hickory forest in Wisconsin with a growing-stock volume of 180 m³/ha.

A. Direct Method

Smith et al. (2003) listed the following coefficients for calculating above-ground biomass (AGB) of oak-hickory in the Northern Lake States:
F = 307.5   G = 0.0748   H = 186.9

Therefore, AGB = F x (G + (1 – exp(-volume/H)))
= 307.5 x (0.0748 + (1 – exp(-180/186.9)))
= 213.1 t/ha

B. BEF Method

As growing-stock volume is < 200 m³/ha, we must calculate the BEF. Oak-hickory is a hardwood forest type.

Therefore, BEF = exp(1.912 – (0.344 x ln GSV))
= exp(1.912 – (0.344 x ln(180)))
= 1.134

Therefore, AGB = GSV x BEF
= 180 x 1.134
= 204.1 t/ha

Example 2: A loblolly pine plantation in Georgia with a growing stock volume of 120 m³/ha.

A. Direct Method

Smith et al. (2003) listed the following coefficients for calculating above-ground biomass (AGB) of planted pine in the Southeastern States:
F = 187.3   G = 0.0662   H = 184.9

Therefore AGB   = F x (G + (1 – exp(-volume/H)))
= 187.3 x (0.0662 + (1 – exp(-120/184.9)))
= 101.8 t/ha

B. BEF Method

Growing stock volume is > 100 m³/ha and the forest type is pine the BEF is 0.81 t/m³.

Therefore, AGB = GSV x BEF
= 120 x 0.81
= 97.2 t/ha

Nontree Vegetation

Herbaceous plants in the forest understory can be measured by simple harvesting techniques in small subplots (about two per tree plot are recommended) for each sample plot. A small frame (circular or square), usually encompassing about 0.25 m^2, can be used. The material inside the frame is cut to ground level, pooled by plot to give a composite sample, and weighed. Well-mixed subsamples are oven-dried to determine dry-to-wet mass ratios. These ratios are used to convert the entire sample to oven-dry mass.

For shrubs and other large nontree vegetation, it is desirable to measure the biomass by destructive harvesting techniques. A small subplot (0.25-4 m^2 depending on the size of the vegetation) is established and all the shrub vegetation is harvested and weighed

If the shrubs are large, an alternative approach is to develop biomass regression equations for local shrubs based on variables such as crown area and height or diameter at base of plant, or another relevant variable, e.g., number of stems in multistemmed shrubs. The equations would then be based on regressions of biomass of the shrub versus a logical combination of the independent variables. This approach is more ambitious and may not be practical for the average inventory.

Below-ground Biomass

Measuring above-ground biomass is relatively established and simple. Measuring below-ground biomass (coarse and fine roots) is time consuming so it is more efficient to apply a regression model to estimate below-ground biomass (living and dead) as a function of above-ground biomass. The following regression models can be used to estimate below-ground biomass (Cairns et al. 1997):

Boreal:

$$BGB = \exp(-1.0587 + 0.8836 \times \ln ABD + 0.1874)$$

Temperate:

$$BGB = \exp(-1.0587 + 0.8836 \times \ln AGB + 0.2840)$$

Tropical:

$$BGB = \exp(-1.0587 + 0.8836 \times \ln AGB)$$

where BGB = below-ground biomass density in tons/hectare (t/ha) and AGB = above-ground biomass density (t/ha)

$n = 151; r^2 = 0.84$

Estimating Change in Below-ground Biomass

The correct use of these equations is important when calculating the increase in carbon in below-ground biomass. For tagged trees in permanent plots, it is not possible to simply calculate the total above-ground biomass at time 1 and time 2, apply the equations, and then divide by the number of years. This approach does not account for ingrowth or mortality trees. Instead, change in below-ground biomass carbon stocks should be calculated by the following method:

1. Calculate above-ground biomass at time 1 using allometric equations and appropriate expansion factors.
2. Calculate increment of biomass accumulation above ground between time 1 and time 2 and add to time 1 to estimate the biomass stock at time 2.
3. Apply the appropriate equation to estimate below-ground biomass at each time interval.
4. Calculate the annual change in stock of biomass below ground as (time 2 below ground - time 1 below ground)/number of years).

Dead Organic Matter

Forest Floor

The forest floor (Table 2) can be sampled directly by simple harvesting techniques in small subplots within each permanent plot (Fig. 3). A circular or square frame, usually encompassing an area of about 0.25 m^2, can be used. If the forest floor is particularly deep as often is the case in western U.S. forests, a smaller frame (0.06 m^2) can be used. If herbaceous material is collected, the forest floor can be collected from the same frames at the same locations. All live vegetation from the sample area is removed carefully with a pair of clippers. Living mosses should be clipped at the base of the green, photosynthetic material. The forest floor along the inner surface of the frame is cut through to separate it from the frame and surrounding soil. The entire volume of the forest floor must be removed carefully from within the confines of the sampling frame down to the top of the mineral soil layer (to distinguish the bottom of the forest floor from the top of the mineral soil, see section on soil organic carbon). All litter within the frame is collected and all samples from the subplots are pooled and weighed. A well-mixed subsample is then collected and placed in a marked bag. The subsample is used to determine oven-dry-to-wet mass ratios to convert the total wet mass to oven-dry mass. Forest-floor samples can be sent to a professional laboratory for drying and weighing.

For the forest floor, amounts of biomass per unit area are given by:

(forest-floor oven-dry weight (g) / sampling frame area (cm^2)) x 100

Where multiplying by 100 converts the units to metric t/ha. Multiplying by 0.5 gives the amount of carbon.

Dead Wood

Dead wood, both standing and on the ground, correlates poorly with any index of stand structure (Harmon et al. 1993). Methods developed for measuring biomass of dead wood and tested in many forest types generally require no more effort than measuring live trees (Harmon and Sexton 1996; Delaney et al. 1998).

A time-efficient method for sampling down dead wood is the line intersect. At least 100 m length of line per plot must be used (Harmon and Sexton 1996). Placing two 50-m sections of line at right angles across the plot center also is a time-efficient approach, though the line can be established as readily as one 100-m length through the plot center. To allow remeasurement of the same "dead wood plot", it is important to accurately record where the line was placed. The diameters of all pieces of wood that intersect the line are measured and the density class noted. A minimum diameter for measurement must be defined—typically 10 cm (Harmon and Sexton 1996). Each piece of dead wood is assigned one of several density classes. The volume per unit area calculated for each density class is:

$$\text{Volume } (m^3/ha) = \pi^2 * [(d1^2 + d2^2 \ldots \ldots dn^2)/8L]$$

Where d1, d2, dn = diameter (cm) of each of the n pieces intersecting the line, and L = the length of the line (100 m recommended; Harmon and Sexton 1996).

Density measurements. Three density classes—sound, intermediate, and rotten—are sufficient. Common practice in the field is to strike the wood with a strong sharp blade. If the blade bounces off, it is sound, if it enters slightly, it is intermediate, if the wood falls apart, it is rotten. Samples of dead wood in each class are then collected to determine their density. Mass of dead wood is then the product of volume per density class (from previous equation) and the wood density for that class. Thus, a key step in this method is classifying the dead wood into its correct class and then sampling a sufficient number of logs in each class to represent the wood densities present. It is advisable to sample at least 10 logs for each density class. In forests with unique plant forms, e.g., early successional species and palms as in tropical forests, it is advisable to treat these as separate groups and sample them in the same way.

The simplest method for estimating the density of dead wood is to obtain a value for the proportion of undecomposed density that each density classes represents. Undecomposed wood densities are widely available in the literature (e.g., U.S. Forest Products Laboratory 1974). Biomass is calculated by multiplying the initial density value by the decomposed proportion by the volume. Heath and Chojnacky (2001) calculated the proportions as 90 percent (sound), 70 percent (intermediate), and 40 percent (rotten) for forests in the Northeast. These proportions can be used, but several samples must be collected to test their validity.

For forest areas with few species and where the rate of decomposition of wood is well known for a given species or forest type, simple decomposition models can be developed locally for estimating the density of the dead wood at different stages of decomposition (Beets et al. 1999). The volume of wood still must be estimated, but density can be estimated based on the model of decomposition. In the following example, the biomass density of dead wood is calculated.

Calculating Biomass Density of Dead Wood

In this example, dead wood is sampled along a 100-m line (line-intersect method) to determine the biomass stock. Diameters and density classes are recorded and a subsample collected to determine density in each of the three density classes (sound, intermediate, and rotten). The following numbers represent the hypothetical results:

13.8 cm: sound
10.7 cm: sound
18.2 cm: sound
10.2 cm: intermediate
11.9 cm: intermediate
56.0 cm: rotten

Densities of subsamples:	Sound:	0.43 t/m^3
	Intermediate:	0.34 t/m^3
	Rotten:	0.19 t/m^3

Volume of sound wood:
$$\pi^2 \times [d1^2 + d2^2 \ldots dn^2/8L]$$
$$\pi^2 \times [13.8^2 + 10.7^2 + 18.2^2/800]$$
$$7.85 \text{ m}^3/\text{ha}$$

Volume of intermediate wood:
$$\pi^2 \times [10.2^2 + 11.9^2/800]$$
$$3.03 \text{ m}^3/\text{ha}$$

Volume of rotten wood:
$$\pi^2 \times [56.0^2/800]$$
$$38.7 \text{ m}^3/\text{ha}$$

Biomass stock = $(7.85 \times 0.43) + (3.03 + 0.34) + (38.7 \times 0.19) = 11.8$ t/ha

Carbon stock $= 11.8 * 0.5 = 5.9$ t C/ha

Standing dead wood can be measured as part of the tree inventory. Standing dead trees should be measured by the same criteria used for live trees. However, measurements that are taken and data that are recorded differ slightly from those for live trees. For example, if the standing dead tree contains branches and twigs and resembles a live tree (except for leaves), this would be indicated on field-data records. From the measurement of its d.b.h., the amount of biomass can be estimated using the appropriate biomass regression equation and subtracting the biomass of leaves (2 to 3 percent of above-ground biomass). However, a dead tree can contain only small and large branches, or only large branches, or no branches. These conditions must be recorded in the field measurements. Branches must be classified in proportion to the size of the standing dead tree so that the total biomass can be reduced accordingly to account for less of the dead tree remaining. When a tree has no branches and is only the bole, its volume can be estimated from measurements of its basal diameter and height and an estimate of its top diameter. The tree's biomass can be estimated using the appropriate density class. In the following examples, the biomass of standing dead wood is calculated.

Calculating Biomass of Standing Dead Wood

1. A tree with no leaves in a mixed hardwood forest with a d.b.h. of 25 cm in sound density class

Use the equation of Jenkins et al. (2003) for mixed hardwood forests with a 3 percent deduction due to the absence of leaves.

y = exp (–2.4800 + 2.4835 x ln(25)) = 248.16 kg x 0.97 = 240.72 kg

As this is the only dead tree measured in a 14-m plot, the mass is multiplied by an expansion factor of 16.24 plots/ha, giving a biomass of 3.91 t/ha (1.96 t C/ha).

2. A sugar maple tree with missing branches (estimated as 15 percent of above-ground biomass). The d.b.h. is 51 cm and the tree is sound.

Use the equation of Jenkins et al. (2003) for hard maple/oak/hickory/beech with a 15 percent deduction for the lack of biomass.

y = exp (–2.0127 + 2.4342 x ln(51)) = 1,916.3 * 0.85 = 1,628.9 kg

As this is the only dead tree measured in a 20-m plot, the mass is multiplied by an expansion factor of 7.96 plots/ha, giving a biomass density of 12.97 t/ha (6.49 t C/ha).

3. A bole with no branches, the height is 15 m, basal diameter is 40 cm, and top diameter is 25 cm. Analysis of a cored sample reveals a wood density of 0.49 g/cm^3.

$$\text{The volume of a truncated cone} = 1/3\pi \times h \times (r_1^2 + r_2^2 + r_1 \times r_2)$$
$$= 1/3\pi \times 1500 \times (20^2 + 12.5^2 + 20 \times 12.5)$$
$$\text{Biomass density} = 1{,}266{,}455 \text{ cm}^3 \times 0.49 \text{ g/cm}^3$$
$$= 620{,}563 \text{ g} = 0.62 \text{ tons}$$

As this is the only dead tree measured in a 14-m plot the mass is multiplied by an expansion factor of 16.24 plots/ha, giving a biomass density of 10.08 t/ha (5.04 t C/ha).

Soil Organic Carbon

To obtain an accurate inventory of organic carbon stocks in the mineral soil[1] or organic soil,[2] three types of variables must be measured: soil depth, soil bulk density (calculated from the oven-dry weight of soil from a known volume of sampled material), and concentrations of organic carbon within the sample. General guidance on sampling and analyzing forest and agricultural soils for estimating carbon stocks are found in Lal et al. (2001) and Robertson et al. (1999).

---

[1]Mineral soil: soil consisting predominantly of and having its properties determined predominantly by mineral matter. Usually contains less than 200 g/kg organic carbon (less than 120-180 g/kg if saturated with water), but may contain an organic surface layer up to 30 cm thick.

[2]Organic soil: soil material that is saturated with water and has 174 or more g/kg organic carbon if the mineral fraction has 500 g/kg or more clay, 116 g/kg organic carbon if the mineral fraction has no clay, or has proportional intermediate contents. If these materials never were saturated with water, they would have 203 or more g/kg organic carbon. Definitions from Technical Guidelines for Voluntary Reporting of Greenhouse Gases 1605(b) Program: http://www.pi.energy.gov/pdf/library/TechnicalGuidelines_March2006.pdf

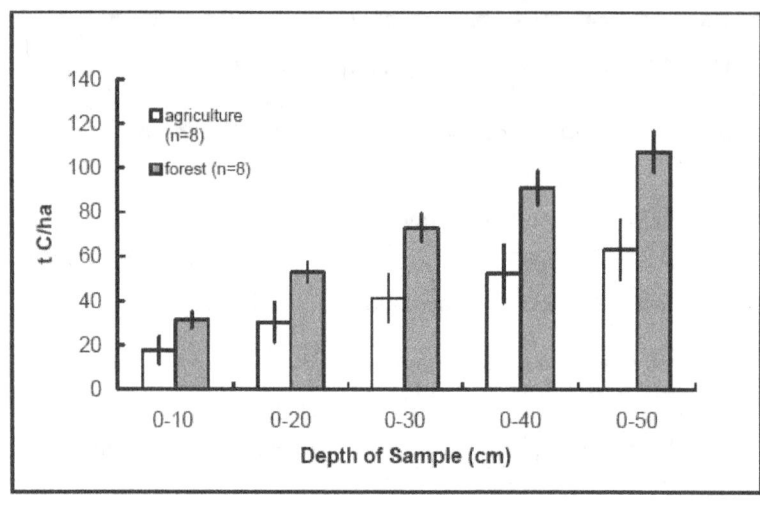

Figure 5.—Mineral soil carbon, forest = 50- to 70-year-old bottomland hardwoods on clay soil, bars = 95 percent confidence intervals.

Tracking changes in soil carbon over time requires that the same *equivalent* mass of soil is measured from one monitoring event to another. Sampling to a fixed depth (equal volumes) can underestimate carbon gains via forestation. As the bulk density generally decreases over time, the same sampled volume contains less of the original soil-mass equivalent. Therefore, rates of accrual estimated from sampling to a fixed depth should be considered *conservative* estimates of soil-carbon accretion.

Where there are no additions of new carbon at greater depth, sampling to greater depth reduces the detectability of change by diluting additions that occur in the upper layers of the soil column. For example, after monitoring 35 years of forest regrowth of loblolly pine in the Calhoun Experimental Forest in South Carolina, Richter et al. (1999) found no significant increase in soil carbon below 7.5 cm. Likewise, in contrasting formerly cultivated and never tilled sites under longleaf pine, Markewitz et al. (2002) found the most notable carbon difference in the upper 10 cm of soil. As hardwood leaf litter is likely to break down and become incorporated into the soil more quickly, and hardwood trees typically produce more roots than pines, inputs of soil carbon are expected to a greater depth—to 40 or 50 centimeters (MacDonald 1999; unpublished data) (Fig. 5).

The forest floor is sampled as described earlier, i.e., exposing the top of the mineral or organic soil. For some soils, it is difficult to distinguish between the bottom of the forest floor and the top of the mineral soil. In such cases, one can refer to standard soil sampling methods, e.g., in Robertson et al. (1999), for tips on how to distinguish the top of mineral soil. Coring tools and liners are available to hold the soil cores of varying lengths, but it often is impractical to use a manually operated, impact-driven, soil-coring tool below about 30 cm. Simple soil corers are effective in many soils, particularly in the deeper soils of the central and southern regions of the United States. Shallow soil pits to about 30 cm also work well and are cost effective. The impact-driven soil coring tool is impractical for collecting deep cores, nor is the use of a truck or trailer-mounted, hydraulically driven soil coring tool practical or cost effective in most forest areas.

Composite sampling is effective in reducing intersample variability. This is done by aggregating a predetermined number of samples (often four) from each collection site in the field, from which one sample is derived for analysis. The resulting *composite* sample captures more of the range of intermicrosite variability in soil carbon.

Sampling Mineral Soil

Concentrations of soil chemicals generally are measured in air-dried soils, while bulk density must be measured in oven-dried soils (to 105 °C). It often is easier to take separate sets of cores when determining bulk density and carbon because the sample preparation differs for each. Fewer cores may be required to accurately estimate bulk density, which generally is less variable than soil-chemical properties.

Using the core sampler method, mineral soil samples are collected from within the area of the sampling frame after the forest floor has been removed. Because the carbon concentration of forest-floor materials is much higher than that of the mineral soil, including even a small amount of surface organic material can result in a serious overestimation of mineral-soil carbon stocks.

Once the soil corer has been inserted into the soil to the desired depth, it is removed from the ground by pulling upward in a smooth vertical motion. The top and bottom (or bottom only depending on the coring tool used) of the core should be trimmed even with the rims. When taking cores for measurements of bulk density, care should be taken to avoid any loss of soil from the cores; if any material is lost, a second sample is needed. All material in the corer should be placed into appropriately labeled sample bags.

The excavation method entails digging a pit that is wide enough to collect the soil to the depth desired. A hand shovel can be used to collect material. The volume of soil from the sides of the pit must approximately equal the volume of a soil corer. It is important to collect material from the entire depth to avoid biasing the sample. Uniform rings can be used to sample the sides of the pit for bulk density, taking care not to compress the soil.

As with forest-floor samples, soil samples can also be sent to a professional lab for analysis. It is important that the selected laboratory follows standard procedures with respect to sample preparation (sieving at 2-mm mesh, grinding, etc.), drying temperatures, method for carbon analysis (dry combustion) and machine calibration and duplicate samples.

In determining bulk density, samples are dried in an oven at 105 °C for a minimum of 48 hr. If the soil contains coarse, rocky fragments, the fragments should be retained and weighed and the weights recorded.

In determining soil carbon, the material is sieved (2-mm sieve) and then mixed thoroughly. In the dry combustion method, a controlled-temperature furnace, e.g., LECO CHN-2000 or equivalent, is used[3]. This method is recommended for determining total carbon in the soil (Nelson and Sommers 1996). Where carbonate minerals may be present, a dry-combustion method that includes use of a LECO RC-412 multicarbon analyzer is preferred (Amacher et al. 2003). Both organic and inorganic forms of carbon can be measured on the same mineral soil sample in one analytical run. An alternative is to remove any carbonates through acid treatment beforehand.

---

[3]The use of trade, firm, or corporation names in this report is for the information and convenience of the reader. Such use does not constitute an official endorsement or approval by the U.S. Department of Agriculture or Forest Service of any product or service to the exclusion of others that may be suitable.

As an alternative to the multicarbon analyzer, the dichromate oxidation method with heating, is acceptable for measuring organic carbon (Nelson and Sommers 1996). The pressure calcimeter method is effective in determining soil carbonates (Sherrod et al. 2002). The classic Walkley-Black method is unacceptable for determining organic carbon in soil due to incomplete wet combustion and other inaccuracies.

The bulk density of the mineral soil core is calculated by:

$$\rho_b = \frac{ODW}{CV - (RF / PD)}$$

Where

ρ_b	=	Bulk density of the < 2mm fraction, (g/cm^3)
ODW	=	Oven-dry mass of fine fraction (<2 mm) in g
CV	=	Core volume (cm^3)
RF	=	Mass of coarse fragments (> 2 mm) in g
PD	=	Density of rock fragments (g/cm^3). This often is given as 2.65 g/cm^3, though the

actual value can be determined by submerging a known mass of coarse fragments in a known volume of water; the displacement gives an estimate of rock volume, which can be used to calculate density.

Data on bulk density and carbon concentrations are used to compute amounts of carbon per unit area.

For the mineral soil, amounts of carbon per unit area are given by:

$$C \ (t/ha) = [(soil \ bulk \ density, \ (g/cm^3) \times soil \ depth \ (cm) \times \% \ C)] \times 100$$

In this equation %C must be expressed as a decimal fraction; for example, 2.2 %C is expressed as 0.022. In the following example, the mass of soil carbon per unit area is calculated.

Calculating Mass of Soil Carbon per Unit Area

Mass of carbon per unit volume is calculated by multiplying carbon concentration (reported as percent mass) times bulk density (g/cm^3). Bulk density equals the oven-dry weight of the soil core divided by the core volume. For example, a core of volume 94.2 cm^3 (1-cm radius x 30-cm length cylinder) with a dry weight 144.06 yields a bulk density of 1.53 g/cm^3. Referencing the sample depth, mass per unit area is calculated, which represents a corresponding volume of soil. Thus,

Volume/ha = 100 m x 100 m x 0.3 m (sample depth) = 3×10^9 cm^3 = 3,000 m^3

Mass/ha = 3×10^9 cm^3 x 1.53 g/cm^3 (bulk density) = 4.586×10^9 g = 4,586 tons

A portion of this volume is occupied by tree roots, which are accounted for separately. However, this fraction tends to be insignificant and is ignored here.

From within the same plot, the corresponding aggregate core analyzed for carbon concentration yields 0.8 percent mass carbon. Mass per unit area, 4,586 t/ha, calculated previously, multiplied by 0.8 percent yields equivalent 36.7 tons of soil carbon/ha. A series of sample calculations of mass soil carbon is tabulated as follows:

Sample weight	Volume	Bulk density	Volume/ha	Mass/ha	Carbon conc.	Mass soil C
g	cm^3	g/cm^3	cm^3	tons	% mass	t/ha
144.06	94.2	1.53	3.E+09	4586	0.80	36.7
126.48	94.2	1.34	3.E+09	4026	0.82	33.0
146.95	94.2	1.56	3.E+09	4678	0.72	33.7
132.20	94.2	1.40	3.E+09	4208	0.90	37.9
147.39	94.2	1.56	3.E+09	4692	0.53	24.9
131.96	94.2	1.40	3.E+09	4200	1.39	58.4
115.95	94.2	1.23	3.E+09	3691	1.22	45.0
133.96	94.2	1.42	3.E+09	4264	1.09	46.5
115.59	94.2	1.23	3.E+09	3679	1.20	44.2
139.03	94.2	1.48	3.E+09	4425	0.76	33.6
					Mean	39.4
					95% CI	6.7

Estimating Net Change and Uncertainty

The type of activity influences how each carbon-stock component (Table 1) is integrated into an estimate of the net change in carbon stock at each monitoring interval. The activities listed in Table 2 can be grouped into two classes. The first class includes those that typically would be implemented on nonforested lands (afforestation, forest restoration, agroforestry, short-rotation biomass energy plantations, and mine-land reclamations). The other class includes activities implemented on existing forested land (forest management and forest preservation). This grouping has implications with respect to how measurements and estimations are integrated to obtain an estimate of the net change in total carbon stocks in the time interval.

Activities on Nonforested Lands

All activities on nonforested lands typically begin on land that initially has low carbon stocks in vegetation (generally less than 2 tons/ha) and variable amounts in the soil. In each case, a sampling regime would be implemented that monitors each carbon-stock component. The task is then combining all the estimates of the carbon stock for each component to obtain an estimate of the net change in total carbon.

Using permanent plots, the carbon stock for living and standing dead trees above and below ground and downed dead wood of individual plots can be monitored through time. Therefore, the change in carbon stocks can be estimated directly at the plot level. In this case, the change in carbon stocks for the different components should be summed within plots to give a per-plot change in carbon stock (t C/ha). Plot-level results are then averaged to obtain the mean and 95-percent confidence intervals. The mean change in carbon stocks per unit area is then multiplied by the area of the project activity to produce an estimate of the total change in carbon. If stratification is used, this approach is repeated for each stratum and then all strata are summed to estimate the total. This total is converted to t CO_2 equivalent by multiplying by 3.67 (the value of 3.67 reflects the ratio of molecular weights between carbon [12] and carbon dioxide [44]).

Soils, forest-floor and nontree vegetation are calculated separately as the statistics, number of sampling plots, and even the sampling interval may differ from the other components. The results from these measurements are analyzed to produce an estimate of the mean and the 95-percent confidence interval. This estimate is added to create a system level mean and 95-percent confidence interval. The total confidence interval is calculated as:

$$\text{Total 95\% CI} = \sqrt{([95\%CI_{veg}]^2 + [95\%CI_{soil}]^2 + [95\%CI_{forest\ floor}]^2 + [95\%CI_{non\text{-}tree\ vegetation}]^2)}$$

Where

$[95\%CI_{veg}]$ = 95-percent confidence interval for vegetation, $[95\%CI_{soil}]$ = 95-percent confidence interval for soil, etc.

If part of the afforested area is harvested, the sampling plots theoretically would monitor the change in live and dead biomass, but they would not monitor the amount going into wood products. As mentioned previously, wood products must be considered because the decrease in live biomass from harvesting does not mean that the equivalent amount of carbon went into the atmosphere—some of it could go into long-lived wood products. To correctly estimate the effects of harvesting on the net change in carbon stocks, the amount of wood biomass going into long-term wood products must be determined. This quantity and its estimated 95-percent confidence interval would then be added to the total change. In the following example, the integration of all the components from permanent plots is given where the initial carbon stocks are of former cropland.

Calculating Net Change for the System

In this example of afforestation activity on 500 ha of former cropland, the baseline for carbon stocks is cropland with an average carbon stock in vegetation of 0.9 t C/ha. The following shows the change in carbon stock between years 1 and 10.

Plot number	Change in carbon stocks			SUM
	Living biomass		Dead organic matter	
	Above-ground: trees	Below-ground	Dead wood	
	t C/ha	t C/ha	t C/ha	t C/ha
Plot 1	12.1	2.4	0.1	14.6
Plot 2	11.5	2.3	0.0	13.8
....	...	...	...	...
....	...	...	...	...
Plot 31	12.6	2.5	0.1	15.1
Plot 32	10.9	2.2	0.1	13.2
			Mean	13.9
			95% CI	2.4
			+ Nontree Vegetation	1.8
			N-T V 95% CI	0.1
			+ Forest Floor	0.2
			F.F. 95% CI	0.1
			+ Soil	0.5
			Soil 95% CI	0.1
			- Baseline Stock on Cropland	0.9
			Baseline 95% CI	0.1
			NET Change in Carbon Stock	15.5

If temporary plots are used to measure changes in carbon stocks, the mean and 95-percent confidence interval of the carbon stock in each component across all plots is calculated at time 1 and time 2. The total carbon stock at each time interval is then estimated by summing the means for each component and the total error is estimated as:

$$\text{Total 95\% CI} = \sqrt{([95\%CI_{c1}]^2 + [95\%CI_{c2}]^2 + \ldots\ldots [95\%CI_{cn}]^2)}$$

Where

$[95\%CI_{c1}]$ = 95-percent confidence interval for component 1, e.g., above-ground biomass, component 2, and so on for all components measured in the plots.

The change in carbon stock is calculated by subtracting the mean carbon stock at time 2 from that at time 1. The confidence interval is calculated as:

$$\text{Total 95\% CI} = \sqrt{[95\%CI_{time1}]^2 + [95\%CI_{time2}]^2}$$

Where

$[95\%CI_{time1}]$ = 95-percent confidence interval for time 1 and $[95\%CI_{time2}]$ = 95-percent confidence interval for time 2.

The net change is calculated similarly for permanent plots by subtracting the initial carbon stocks (nearly zero if afforestation occurs on former cropland) from the carbon stocks that accrued at the time of measurement. Finally, the total carbon-stock change per unit area is multiplied by the total area to produce the estimated total change in carbon and confidence interval for the area.

In this section we have focused on an activity with a single stratum. If the activity contained multiple strata, each would be calculated separately as described. Once the area-based carbon dioxide equivalents and confidence levels are calculated for each stratum, the values can be combined to obtain total carbon stock or stock change for all carbon pools in all strata. The new confidence interval for the combined strata would be estimated as:

$$\text{Total 95\% CI} = \sqrt{[95\%CI_{s1}]^2 + [95\%CI_{s2}]^2 + \ldots \ldots \ldots [95\%CI_{sn}]^2}$$

Where

$[95\%CI_{s1}]$ = 95-percent confidence interval for strata 1, strata 2, and so on for all strata measured in the project).

The methods presented here for calculating uncertainty in reported values are known as "error propagation." Error propagation is simple and robust. However, these methods should be used with caution where there are:

- Strong correlations between datasets (there is a significant covariance), or
- Uncertainties exceed 100 percent

In such cases it is statistically more appropriate to use a Monte Carlo analysis.[4] In practice the difference in results attained through the two methods are small unless correlations and/or uncertainties are very high.

Guidance on analyzing uncertainty and propagating errors is found in Annex 1 of the "IPCC Good Practice Guidance and Uncertainty Management in National Greenhouse Gas Inventories" (2000; http://www.ipcc-nggip.iges.or.jp/public/gp/english/).

---

[4]The principle of Monte Carlo analyses is to perform the summing of uncertainties many times each time with the uncertain stocks or increments chosen randomly by Monte Carlo software from within the distribution of uncertainties input initially by the user. Examples of Monte Carlo software include Simetar, @Risk, and Crystal Ball (www.simetar.com, www.palisade.com/html/risk.asp, www.crystalball.com).

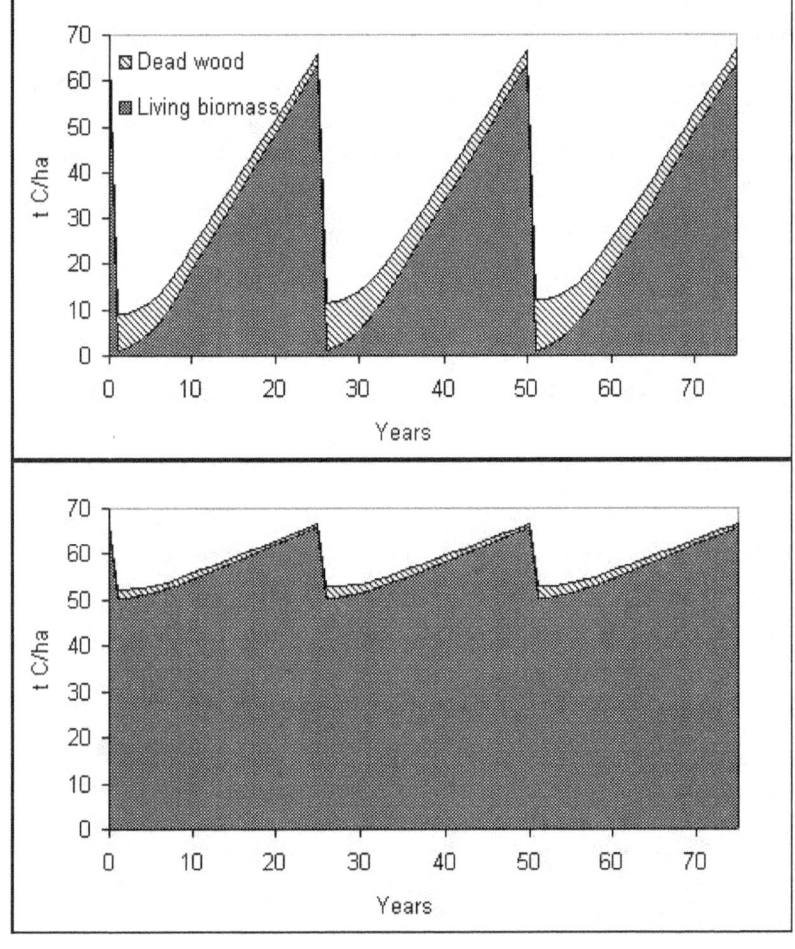

Figure 6.—Carbon stocks associated with (top) complete harvest of forest followed by 25-year even-age management and (bottom) selective harvest of a similar forest.

Activities on Forested Lands

Forest management consists of alternating periods of harvest and regrowth such that carbon stocks in forest biomass vary over time (Fig. 6). Changes in management practices also can increase carbon storage by changing the timing or intensity of harvest, reducing damage to the residual stand through more efficient logging practices, switching from clearcutting to selective harvesting, or by creating or widening riparian buffer zones.

Initially, it is important to consider which carbon pools are important in forest management. Live vegetation, dead wood, and wood products are obvious examples. With the examples in Figure 6, the amount of dead wood could increase over time with a subsequent harvest. The amount of dead wood that accumulates through time is a function of the amount of slash left behind and the rate of decomposition of that slash. The larger the amount of slash and the slower the rate of decomposition, the larger the amount that accumulates. For preservation of mature forests, the dead-wood carbon stock can be highly significant. Measuring soil organic carbon is marginally beneficial at best in forest management. Soil carbon may be reduced slightly immediately following harvest (Laiho et al. 2002, Carter et al. 2002), though any losses will be regained as the succeeding forest regrows with accompanying soil organic-matter inputs (Carter et al. 2002). The relative difference in postharvest effects on soil carbon among different harvest intensities is slight and often undetectable (Carter et al. 2002). As a result, additional soil sampling on projects on forested lands is not recommended.

An important additional consideration is storage of carbon in long-term wood products. Timber extracted from the forest is not immediately emitted to the atmosphere but is stored in wood products, often for many years. Guidance on wood products is included in the appendix to the technical guidelines for the 1605(b) process and in a publication by Smith et al. (2006).

Differences in the effects of clearcutting versus selective harvests on forest-ecosystem carbon stocks (Figure 6) affects the accuracy and precision of measuring and monitoring changes over time. There are two alternative methodologies for monitoring changes in carbon stocks: direct and indirect measurement.

Direct Measurement

Where the activity includes clearcutting, the simplest approach is to install sample plots and monitor the changes in carbon stocks as described previously. As shown in Figure 6, there will be periods of carbon accumulation and a period of carbon loss resulting in positive and negative changes in carbon stocks. With a well designed sampling regime, remeasurements will reveal shifts of preharvest living biomass to the dead wood pool (logging slash and collateral mortality) and subsequent decomposition over time, as well as regrowth, after harvest. Mean total carbon stocks and 95-percent confidence intervals are calculated in the same way as for activities on nonforested lands.

Indirect Measurement

For selective cutting where harvest intensity per hectare is low, the required number of plots to capture the variation in harvested areas could be so large as to make measurement neither practical nor cost effective. In this case, it is possible to use targeted measurements plus the statistics of the relevant logging activity. It is more appropriate to measure the change in live biomass due to harvesting directly. The change in live biomass caused by logging is a result of the extraction of timber and damage to residual trees. Calculating carbon gains and losses by indirect measurement typically requires information on:

- Total volume removed.
- Area damaged (converted from living to dead biomass) per cubic meter removed.
- Amount of slash and damage to residual stand per volume removed.
- Rate of regrowth in the harvested areas relative to nonharvested areas (relative rate of carbon accumulation).
- Decomposition rates of slash.

The change in carbon stocks using this approach is calculated as:

Δ live biomass C + Δ dead biomass C

Where

Δ is the change in carbon of live biomass and dead biomass caused by timber harvesting. Estimates of each term can be made annually or over longer periods.

The change in live biomass caused by logging is a result of the extraction of timber, slash from the harvested tree, and damage to residual trees, all of which will reduce live biomass or represent a negative quantity after harvest.

Δ live biomass C = ([biomass C from logging damage + C in timber extracted])

An additional component of the analysis is the relative rate of carbon accumulation during regrowth that applies to areas affected by timber extraction. This could be faster or slower in a logged than in an unlogged area. A stand is thinned to enhance the growth rate of the desired trees. However, from a stand perspective, the rate of carbon accumulation can be slower, faster, or the same because trees have been removed and damaged in the logged gaps. The default assumption is equal growth rates between logged and unlogged areas. For example, in a mixed tropical forest in Bolivia, measurements of nearly 100 paired logged and unlogged plots over 4 years showed no significant difference in carbon accumulation rates between the two sets of plots (unpublished data).

In estimating the amount of damaged and dead biomass produced in the logging operations, field plots are established around a harvested tree(s). The plot usually has dimensions equivalent to the gap of the harvested tree, which can be estimated by GPS. Data are collected on the initial diameter and height of the harvested tree, and the amount of volume removed is measured, as is the diameter of all trees that were severely damaged (snapped or uprooted) and presumed dead. Measurements in 100 logged tree gaps ensure adequate precision. The measurements are then combined to produce a ratio of total amount of live biomass converted to dead biomass per unit mass of timber extracted.

The carbon in extracted timber enters wood products where it can remain fixed for a prolonged period. Guidance is available for tracking carbon in wood products (Smith et al. 2006).

Δ dead biomass C = (dead biomass from logging damage and slash times the decomposition rate)

The slash and damaged wood are assumed to enter the dead wood pool, where they begin to decompose. Each year, dead wood is added from harvesting, though some is lost each year due to decomposition and resulting carbon emissions. Decomposition of dead wood is modeled as a simple exponential function based on mass of dead wood and a decomposition coefficient (proportion decomposed per year). Decomposition coefficients for major U.S. forest types are given in Table 5. The change in carbon stocks of the slash and damaged wood can be measured in the field, but this tends to be time consuming and costly. Mean total changes in carbon stocks and 95-percent confidence intervals can be calculated in the same way as described earlier.

Table 5.—Decomposition rate constants and half lives for down dead wood, by region and forest type

Region	Forest type	Decomposition rate[a]	Half life
		Year⁻¹	*Years*
Pacific Northwest	Douglas-fir	0.022	31.5
	Spruce-fir	0.028	24.8
	Hemlock-spruce	0.031	22.4
	Lodgepole pine	0.041	16.9
	Hardwoods	0.082	8.5
	Ponderosa pine	0.017	40.8
	Redwoods	0.014	49.5
Rocky Mountains	Douglas-fir	0.022	31.5
	Ponderosa pine	0.017	40.8
	Spruce-fir	0.014	49.5
	Larch	0.022	31.5
	Lodgepole pine	0.023	30.1
South	Oak-hickory	0.075	9.2
	Oak-pine	0.060	11.6
	Bottomland hardwood	0.112	6.2
	Natural pine	0.056	12.4
	Planted pine	0.056	12.4
Northeast	White/red pine	0.042	16.5
	Spruce-fir	0.042	16.5
	Oak-hickory	0.075	9.2
	Maple-beech-birch	0.062	11.2
North Central	White/red pine	0.042	16.5
	Spruce-fir	0.042	16.5
	Maple-beech	0.082	8.5
	Aspen-birch	0.082	8.5
	Bottomland hardwood	0.112	6.2
	Oak-hickory	0.060	11.6

[a]From Turner et al. 1993.

QUALITY ASSURANCE AND QUALITY CONTROL (QA/QC)

Measuring and monitoring requires provisions for quality assurance (QA) and quality control (QC) to be implemented via a QA/QC plan to ensure that the reported carbon units are reliable and meet minimum measurement standards. The plan should become part of the documentation and include procedures for: (1) collecting reliable field measurements; (2) verifying laboratory procedures; (3) verifying data entry and analysis techniques; and (4) data maintenance and archiving.

QA/QC for Field Measurements

Collecting reliable field measurements is an important step in the QA plan. Those responsible for the carbon measurement should be fully trained in all aspects of field data collection and data analyses. It is wise to prepare Standard Operating Procedures (SOP) for each step of field carbon measurements. These SOPs should detail all phases of the field measurements so that the measurements can be repeated. A document should be produced and filed with the project documents verifying that all QA/QC steps have been taken.

Field crews should receive extensive training and be fully cognizant of all procedures and the importance of collecting accurate data. An audit program for field measurements and sampling should be established. A typical audit program consists of three types of checks. During a *hot check*, auditors observe members of the field crew during data collection on a field plot (this is primarily for training purposes). *Cold checks* occur when field crews are not present for the audit. *Blind checks* represent the complete remeasurement of a plot by the auditors. Hot checks allow the correction of errors in techniques. Measurement variance can be calculated through blind checks. When fieldwork is completed, about 10 percent of the plots should be checked independently. Field data collected at this stage can be compared with the original data, and errors should be corrected and recorded. Errors can be expressed as a percentage of all plots that have been rechecked to provide an estimate of the measurement error.

QA/QC for Laboratory Measurements

The SOPs also should be prepared by the operating entity and followed for each part of the analyses. Typical steps for the SOP for laboratory measurements include calibrating combustion instruments for measuring total carbon or carbon forms using commercially available certified carbon standards. Similarly, all balances for measuring dry weights should be calibrated periodically against known weights. Fine-scale balances should be calibrated by the manufacturer. Where possible, 10 to 20 percent of the samples should be reanalyzed/reweighed to produce an error estimate. If a laboratory perform these steps, be sure to obtain a record of the procedure(s).

QA/QC for Data Entry

The proper entry of data into analysis spreadsheets is required. This step may be redundant if the field data are collected in an electronic format. Ongoing communication between all personnel involved in measuring and analyzing data is critical for resolving apparent anomalies before final analysis of the monitoring data is completed. If there are any anomalies that cannot be resolved, the plot should not be used in the analysis. Errors can be reduced if entered data are compared with independent data.

QA/QC for Data Archiving

Because of the relatively long-term nature of forestry activities, data archiving (maintenance and storage) is important and should include the following steps:

- Original copies of the field measurement (data sheets or electronic files) and laboratory data should be maintained in original form, placed on electronic media, and stored in a secure location.
- Copies of all data analyses, models, the final estimate of the amount of carbon sequestered, GIS products, and a copy of the measuring and monitoring reports also should all be stored in a secure location (preferably offsite).

Given the period for reporting and the pace of production of updated versions of software and new hardware for storing data, electronic copies of the data and report should be updated periodically or converted to a format that can be accessed by new or updated software.

LITERATURE CITED

Amacher, M.C.; O'Neill, K.P.; Dressbach, R.; Palmer, C. 2003. **Forest inventory and analysis manual of soil analysis methods.** [Online publication]. Available on-line at http://nrs.fs.fed.us/fia/topics/soils/documents/FIA.P3.Soils.Lab.Manual.2003.pdf. [Accessed August, 21, 2007].

Avery T.E.; Burkhart H.E., eds. 1983. **Forest measurements. 3rd ed.** New York: McGraw-Hill.

Beets, P.N.; Robertson, K.A.; Ford-Robertson, J.B.; Gordon, J.; Maclaren, J.P. 1999. **Description and validation of C change: a model for simulating carbon content in managed *Pinus radiata* stands.** New Zealand Journal of Forestry Science. 29: 409-427.

Birdsey, Richard A. 2006. **Carbon accounting rules and guidelines for the United States forest sector.** Journal of Environmental Quality. 35: 1518:1524.

Brown, S. 1997. **Estimating biomass and biomass change of tropical forests: A primer.** FAO For. Pap. 134. Rome: Food and Agriculture Organization of the United Nations. 55 p. [Online publication].

Brown, S. 2002. **Measuring carbon in forests: current status and future challenges.** Environmental Pollution. 116: 363-372.

Brown, S.; Gillespie, A.J.R.; Lugo, A.E. 1989. **Biomass estimation methods for Tropical forests with applications to forest inventory data.** Forest Science. 35: 881-902.

Brown, S.; Masera, O.; Sathaye; J. 2000. **Project-based activities.** In: Watson, R.; Noble, I.; Bolin, B.; Ravindranath, N. H.; Verardo, D. J.; Dokken, D. J., eds. Land use, land-use change, and forestry. Special report to the Intergovernmental Panel on Climate Change. Cambridge. UK: Cambridge University Press: 283-338.

Brown, S.L.; Schroeder, P.E. 1999. **Spatial patterns of aboveground production and mortality of woody biomass for eastern US forests.** Ecological Applications 9: 968-980. [Errata: Brown, S.L., Schroeder, P.E. 2000. Ecological Applications 10: 937].

Cairns, M.A.; Brown, S.; Helmer, E.H.; Baumgardner, G.A. 1997. **Root biomass allocation in the world's upland forests.** Oecologia 111: 1-11.

Carter, M.C.; Dean; T.J.: Zhou, M.; Messina, M.J.; Wang, Z. 2002. **Short-term changes in soil C, N, and biota following harvesting and regeneration of loblolly pine (*Pinus taeda* L.).** Forest Ecology and Management. 164: 67-88.

Clark, D.A.; Brown, S.; Kicklighter, D.W.; Chambers, J.Q.; Thomlinson, J.R.; Ni, Jian. 2001. **Measuring net primary production in forests: concepts and field methods.** Ecological Applications. 11: 356-370.

Dawkins, H.C. 1957. **Some results of stratified random sampling of tropical high forest.** Seventh British Commonwealth Forestry Conference. 7 (iii): 1-12.

Delaney, M.; Brown, S.; Lugo, A. E.; Torres-Lezama, A.; Bello Quintero, N. 1998. **The quantity and turnover of dead wood in permanent forest plots in six life zones of Venezuela.** Biotropica. 30: 2-11.

Fang, J.Y.; Wang, G.; Liu, G.H.; Xu, S.L. 1998. **Forest biomass of China: an estimation based on biomass-volume relationships.** Ecological Applications. 8: 1084-1091.

Forest Products Laboratory. 1974. **Wood handbook: Wood as an engineering material.** USDA Agric. Handb. 72 (rev.). Washington DC: U.S. Department of Agriculture.

Freese, F. 1962. **Elementary forest sampling.** Agric. Handb. Handbook 232. Washington, DC: U.S. Department of Agriculture. 91 p.

Harmon, M. E.; Brown, S.; Gower, S.T. 1993. **Consequences of tree mortality to the global carbon cycle.** In: Vinson, T. S.; Kolchugina, T. P., eds. Carbon cycling in boreal and subartic ecosystems: biospheric response and feedbacks to global climate change: symposium proceedings. Corvallis, OR: U.S. Environmental Protection Agency: 167-176.

Harmon, M.E.; Sexton, J. 1996. **Guidelines for measurements of woody detritus in forest ecosystems.** LTER Publ. 20. [Online publication].

Heath, Linda S.; Chojnacky, David C. 2001. **Down dead wood statistics for Maine timberlands, 1995.** Resour. Bull. NE-150. Newtown Square, PA: U.S. Department of Agriculture, Forest Service, Northeastern Research Station. 80 p.

Intergovernmental Panel on Climate Change. 2000. **Good practice guidance and uncertainty management in national greenhouse gas inventories.** [Online publication]. http://www.ipcc-nggip.iges.or.jp/public/gp/english. [Accessed August, 20, 2007].

Jenkins, J.C.; Chojnacky, D.C.; Heath, L.S.; Birdsey, R.A. 2003. **National-scale biomass estimation for United States tree species.** Forest Science. 49: 12-35.

Jenkins, Jennifer C.; Chojnacky, David C.; Heath, Linda S.; Birdsey, Richard A. 2004. **Comprehensive database of diameter-based biomass regressions for North American tree species.** Gen. Tech. Rep. NE-319. Newtown Square, PA: U.S. Department of Agriculture, Forest Service, Northeastern Research Station. 45 p. [1 CD-ROM]. http://www.fs.fed.us/ne/durham/4104/papers/ne_gtr319_jenkins_and_others.pdf

Laiho, R.; Sanchez, F.; Tiarks, A.; Dougherty, P.M.; Trettin. C.C. 2002. **Impacts of intensive forestry on early rotation trends in site carbon pools in the southeastern US.** Forest Ecology and Management. 174: 177-189.

Lal, R.; Kimble, J.M.; Follett, R.F.; Stewart, B.A., eds. 2001. **Assessment methods for soil carbon.** Boca Raton, FL: Lewis Publishers.

MacDonald, C. 1999. **Dynamics of soil organic carbon content due to reforestation of bottomland hardwood forests on marginal farmland in the Mississippi River Valley.** Nacodoches, TX: Stephen F. Austin State University. M.S. Thesis.

Markewitz, D.; Sartori, F.; Craft, C. 2002. **Soil change and carbon storage in longleaf pine stands planted on marginal agricultural lands.** Ecological Applications. 12: 1276-1285.

Nelson, D.W.; Sommers, L.E. 1996. **Total carbon, organic carbon, and organic matter.** In: D.L. Sparks et al. eds. Methods of soil analysis. Madison, WI: Soil Science Society of America: 961-1010.

Pastor, J.; Aber, J.D.; Melillo, J.M. 1984. **Biomass prediction using generalized allometric regressions for some northeast tree species.** Forest Ecology and Management. 7: 265-274.

Richter, D.R.; Markewitz, D.; Trumbore, S.E.; Wells, C.G. 1999. **Rapid accumulation and turnover of soil carbon in a reestablishing forest.** Nature. 400: 56-58.

Robertson, G.P.; Coleman, D.C.; Bledsoe, C.S.; Sollins, P. 1999. **Standard methods for long-term ecological research.** Oxford, U.K: Oxford University Press.

Schroeder, P.; Brown, S.; Mo, J.; Birdsey, R,; Cieszewski, C. 1997. **Biomass estimation for temperate broadleaf forests of the United States using inventory data.** Forest Science. 43: 424-434.

Sherrod, L.A.; Dunn, G.; Peterson, G.A.; Kolberg, R.L. 2002. **Inorganic carbon analysis by modified pressure calcimeter method.** Soil Science Society of America Journal. 66: 299-305.

Smith, J.E.; Heath, L.S.; Jenkins, J.C. 2003. **Forest volume-to-biomass models and estimates of mass for live and standing dead trees of U.S. forests.** Gen. Tech. Rep. NE-298. Newtown Square, PA: U.S. Department of Agriculture, Forest Service, Northeastern Research Station. 57 p.

Smith, James E.; Heath, Linda S.; Skog, Kenneth E.; Birdsey, Richard A. 2006. **Methods for calculating forest ecosystem and harvested carbon with standard estimates for forest types of the United States.** Gen. Tech. Rep. NE-343. Newtown Square, PA: U.S. Department of Agriculture, Forest Service, Northeastern Research Station. 216 p.

Sokal, R.R.; Rohlf, F.J. 1995. **Biometry: the principles and practice of statistics in biological research.** 3rd ed. New York: W. H. Freeman and Co.

Turner, D.P.; Lee, J.J.; Koerper, G.J.; Barker, J.R. 1993. **The forest sector carbon budget of the United States: carbon pools and flux under alternative policy options.** EPA/600/3-93/093. Washington, DC: U.S. Environmental Protection Agency.

Zar, J.H. 1996. **Biostatistical analysis.** Englewood Cliffs, Prentice Hall.

www.ingramcontent.com/pod-product-compliance
Lightning Source LLC
Chambersburg PA
CBHW080622290526
45790CB00007B/2889